DIVORCE WITH SANITY

A practical guide to divorce with dignity, self-respect, and cooperation.

RICHARD S RABBIN
Family Law Attorney

Published by Richard S Rabbin
Thousand Oaks, California, USA
rsrabbin@sbcglobal.net
http://www.richardsrabbin.com

Copyright © Richard S Rabbin 2011

All rights reserved. No part of this publication may be reproduced, distributed, or transmitted in any form or by any means, including photocopying, recording, or other electronic or mechanical methods, without the prior written permission of the author, except in the case of brief quotations embodied in critical reviews and certain other noncommercial uses permitted by copyright law.

Printed in the United States of America

First Printing, 2011

Book cover artwork by Cathryn Mann
www.catmannstudios.com

Book cover creation and interior design by Jane Green
www.everlastingmagicdesign.com

ISBN: 978-0-615-52287-6

This book is intended as a reference guide only. The information presented here is designed to help you make informed decisions about separation and divorce. It is not intended as a substitute for services provided by a lawyer or legal representative.

I am dedicating this book to Dr. Leonard Diamond, Phd., who passed away after helping me revise this manuscript but before it could be published. His help in revising this manuscript was invaluable and very much appreciated. Leonard was a psychologist who was very well known for the work he did with families and children in divorce. This manuscript has been in the works for many years, and several years ago Leonard wanted to dedicate this book as follows: To all of our children whom we dearly love: Courtney, Dusty, Jennifer, Juliet, Katie, Keith, Shannon. In honor of Leonard, I include this dedication.

I would also like to acknowledge and thank the many clients who have hired me to help them with their family law cases. Without these people and the experiences we have had together, this book could not have come into being. I have been fortunate to represent many fine people who were having a tough time in their lives. Many of these clients have taught me about human nature and the wonderful world of relationships. Some continue to be my friends. I also would like to acknowledge the attorneys I have dealt with and judges before whom I have appeared. Despite the reputation of the profession in some circles, I can assure you that there are many lawyers who really do have their clients' best interests at heart and work very hard to resolve cases out of court. Judges who sit in Family Law Courts have a tough job and most all of them that I have appeared before have done their very best to come to a fair result for the litigants in their courtrooms.

I would also like to thank my sister Gina Rabbin and my brother Robert Rabbin for helping me in the publishing of this book, and my wife Sally Pittman-Rabbin for her time spent editing the manuscript. I am also very grateful to Jane Green and her marvelous guidance in the publication of my first book.

Table of Contents

Introduction i

CHAPTER 1
DO I REALLY WANT A DIVORCE
OR DO I WANT REVENGE? 1

CHAPTER 2
TALKING TO YOUR SPOUSE ABOUT DIVORCE 23

CHAPTER 3
CHOOSING AN ATTORNEY (INCLUDING COLLABORATIVE) 47

CHAPTER 4
LEGAL PROCEDURES FOR DIVORCE 63

CHAPTER 5
MEDIATING YOUR DIVORCE 85

CHAPTER 6
DIVORCE WITHOUT CHILDREN 95

CHAPTER 7
DIVORCE WITH CHILDREN 107

CHAPTER 8
MAINTAINING A WORKING RELATIONSHIP 131

CHAPTER 9
DIVORCE IN A NEW AGE 151

CHAPTER 10
REFLECTIONS ON RELATIONSHIPS 165

About the Author 174

Introduction

Although statistical studies will differ from one geographical area to another area, most current researchers in the field of marriage can agree that at least one-half (and frequently more) of all of the marriages in the United States are doomed to end in divorce. The process of divorce is always a significant emotional trauma which impacts all of the direct participants, including children, as well as peripheral participants such as family members and friends. In fact, it also very definitely impacts long-term family friends who are now faced with the terrible prospect of having to choose sides, especially if the divorcing couple is bitter and hostile.

This book is written for those who are in the throes of dissolving their marriages or for those who are beginning to think that this might be their best option to pursue. The data on which this book is based arises from the first-hand, in-depth, real-world experiences of the author. I have worked in the field of divorce and child custody for over thirty years, as has Dr. Leonard Diamond who has added his psychological view points to this book. His participation has added this depth and, as such, you will note that many times I use the word "we" instead of "I", due to this input. We have witnessed and experienced the intense upset, the confusion, the agitation, the trauma and the pain of divorce. In addition to the horror of the relationship breaking down, the divorcing individuals are also faced with a vague and unstructured legal system in which they must operate. The language of the law and the logic of the law will certainly seem foreign and confusing. The complex courtroom procedures and the negotiations that are always necessary may often be experienced as highly agitating, hostile, adversarial and very slow moving.

The initial goal in this writing is to offer clarity to the whole process, to assist the reader in making better-educated decisions, and see this divorce as a tool for enhanced personal growth and expansion. I offer ways to make this process easier for you to navigate through. The next goal is to prepare you for the complexities and vagaries of the legal and psychological issues so that there will be no major surprises. You will also learn the relationship between the legal process and your emotional reactions which will help you to move through the system more expediently.

Next to parenting, marriage is most definitely the single most important relationship that one faces in our society. Marriage may take place hastily as a reaction to a bio-chemical process over which we have no control. It may also take place after long periods of decision-making, testing each other and emotional trials by fire. People handle the process utilized in the establishment of relationships very differently. However, the one point that we can all agree upon is that at the time that those important vows are spoken, each of us usually believes wholeheartedly that this relationship is like no other, that it was made in Heaven and that it will truly continue until "death do us part." There is unconditional love and caring, unconditional trust and giving. Almost every person who has ever described their marriage has said that without question, they wholeheartedly believed that this relationship was destined to last forever. If this is the case, why then do we often spend so little time examining and comparing our definitions of what goes into a successful relationship before we marry?

Marriage creates a legal and psychological bond which initially feels like it cannot be broken. However, even though it feels strong and unbreakable, we know that marriage is actually a very fragile relationship. The marriage bond is forever severed by divorce after the relationship has come to a grinding halt. Establishing the bond initially may be very difficult and often painful. Severing the bond through divorce is equally painful if not more and it dramatically changes our lives once again and forever. If one is willing to thoroughly examine the complexities of the marital relationship as well as the reasons for dissolving it, it can become an easier and more understandable process for all concerned. This can also lead to a more fulfilling and satisfying future where similar past errors are never repeated. This is the opportunity for personal emotional growth. The procedures which will be introduced and discussed in this book will enable the divorcing individual to become emotionally healthier, more competent with the process and more fulfilled as a person.

The experience of going through a divorce can best be likened to a grief experience over a death in the family. It is no wonder that at the beginning of the divorce we are always so fragile emotionally. Unfortunately, it is at this time that we are forced to make extremely important choices which will inevitably affect our futures. <u>The first and most important choice is to find an appropriately trained, understanding, insightful and competent attorney who will actively help to guide you through the legal system.</u> This system is composed of a unique set of rules, behaviors and actions which often do not seem fair and which frequently demand that you enter into a win-lose situation. You are forced to participate in this adversarial fight against someone you have shared a bed with, eaten with, raised children with, celebrated holidays with, and cared about for many years. Unfamiliar and complex fears enter the consciousness. These fears center on the areas of rejection, abandonment, lack of self-esteem, financial issues and other very important concerns.

We cannot count on receiving any substantial assistance from Judges or from the legal system. Because the dockets are so full and the courtrooms are so crowded and the judges have so many family issues over which they must officiate, they urge the mediators and attorneys to attempt settlements and make agreements. Attorneys are trained to offer the best legal advice they can and to represent their clients to the best of their abilities. The mediators or conciliators in the legal system also urge us to make compromises, but, at the same time, they place obstacles in our way because we are not familiar with the legal issues and the procedures necessary. Therefore, the question still remains as to how we can get some clear perspective on the issues and how we can allow the emotional-psychological experience to mesh and resolve with the legal experience. This process is another of the goals inherent in this writing. The author wishes to separate out the issues to be examined, make them more understandable, and present a more complete and less complex process which will assist in decision-making. The emotional issues must also be addressed correctly in order to experience a significant comfort level once the decisions have been made. As an example of how information helps the process, let us look at a potentially explosive circumstance that happens regularly. Recently, while in court, a man was heard to complain bitterly to his attorney that his wife's attorney was making him do so much work and research with regard to their financial situation. He was very angered because he was being honest and up front and he felt that his wife and her attorney were accusing him of hiding money. He was calling the other attorney many names and then allowing his anger to slide over to his spouse. The feelings began to escalate for this man into an almost debilitating emotional experience. He was turning red and smoke was coming out of his ears. His attorney, seeing what was happening, took the time in a very calm and supportive manner, to make him understand. He said, "She's not after you. Of course she wants you to supply copies of all of the checkbook ledgers. She's not saying that you are a bad guy. She is doing her job for her client just as thoroughly as I would do. Her thoroughness is good for us all and for the case, because when we supply all the data they want, we will be able to understand the issues and we will all agree on the same set of numbers. This is the kind of work that has to be done. It's just good lawyering." This type of explanation and insight is most helpful when it feels like the world is crashing down around you.

Often, there are children involved. Many adults take the position that they should stay together and pretend that all is well, 'for the sake of the children'. What they do not know is that the children are usually very aware, insightful and sophisticated as to their own needs and the needs and motives of their parents. When we shut the children out of the situation and give them no information or poor and distorted information, they suffer a great deal. In addition, this then allows the adults to use the children as leverage or as 'pawns' against each other. Children become more like the tools of divorce than the real people that they are. It is imperative that we learn to address these issues and pay attention to the needs of the children.

In this book there are numerous case histories to illustrate both good and bad approaches. It is worthwhile to study how people have dealt with divorce in the past, where they have made the most errors and how they could have made their divorce easier on themselves and on all concerned. These examples will cover both specifically unique situations as well as the very ordinary and mundane situations (if, in fact, that does exist in the area of divorce). We will look over the shoulder of the family law process as it tries to divide up property, establish guidelines for family, spousal, and child support as well as issues of custody and visitation. In this way, you will be able to see some of the successful ways to operate as well as many of the pitfalls. We will look at different approaches you might take to examine your own marriage and divorce and still maintain a healthy, productive, ongoing working relationship with your ex-spouse. In addition, the very important areas of physical and mental spousal abuse will be exposed and studied. These information-filled case histories will enable you to see healthier avenues of approach and better emotional outlooks to the problems which you will inevitably face. You will also be given a general overview of divorce law, practical suggestions on choosing an appropriate and competent attorney and how to deal with your problems if you cannot afford an attorney. The new and developing area of Collaborative Law will be discussed so that you can be informed as to the possibility of having your own attorney but work closely in a non-adversarial way with your spouse and his/her attorney. You will be instructed as to the role of the psychologist and mediators so that you can select competent mental health professionals as well. Since the divorce laws carry so many inherent difficulties, which we have studied, we can take the liberty in this book of offering a somewhat different and absolutely more humane system designed specifically to make it easier on divorcing couples. These thoughts will be offered to you as well as a chapter on the process of mediation.

    I hope that this book will be read carefully for it will serve to benefit your life and your struggle. You will be presented with new and different attitudes and ideas since it is our desire that the process of divorce not take such an emotional toll. It is the ideal that spouses, children, family and friends, will suffer as little irreversible damage as possible. It really is possible to have an "easier divorce".

CHAPTER 1
DO I REALLY WANT A DIVORCE OR DO I WANT REVENGE?

Attorneys who practice family law as their major emphasis may often find themselves placed in very uncomfortable positions. They may easily be forced into unhealthy, foolish and inappropriate court situations because they are unlucky enough to have a very angry, vengeful, disturbed or misguided client. As an excellent example of this type of situation, the author was representing an individual who was absolutely determined to fight to the death over every piece of property, every asset, and every debt, no matter how large or small, in a very angry divorce situation. Because there were no children involved, this actually should have allowed the parties to settle their issues and just walk away from each other. Instead of acting in a rational and competent manner, both parties became highly emotionally invested in the very minimal property that was purchased during the marriage. The client insisted that his attorney make a life and death dedicated effort to get him certain property. Was it a favorite family heirloom in which he was interested? Was it an expensive piece of furniture? On the contrary, against his attorney's strong admonition, the client loudly and insistently instructed, "I don't care what the consequences might be. I want you to get in there and fight. You have to get me that Popeye magnet she has in the house. I want it! I expect you to get it for me! I will have it and that's that!" This certainly sounds stupid, but it is true! The attorney, his mouth open to its fullest extent, could not even argue this point since the client had made himself abundantly clear. Even after the attorney pointed out to the client that this item was easily replaceable by the client for a very small fraction of the attorney's hourly fee, the client was steadfast in his desire to have it. He wanted only THIS magnet and no other. Why? Because he wanted revenge, and, for some bizarre reason known only to himself, he felt that by being able to take this particular piece of property from his ex-wife, he would have his revenge. He did not care about the financial cost or the psychological cost, just so long as his ex-wife was not able to keep this property.

We have seen clients who have forced their attorneys to fight for purple towels, potty-chairs and broken television sets. This demonstrates very well how a relatively simple and straightforward divorce can be turned into a situation of intense anger build-up and resentments by the participants. Be aware also that others fuel this fire. It is not unheard of for family members and even less scrupulous attorneys to try and move the husband and wife in this direction for some personal reason. Ask yourself the question: "Do I want to kill, spindle and mutilate or do I want to end this marriage and get my divorce as fast as I can?" Be aware of these options and of your real needs. Perhaps if this question is made public by saying it out loud, it will help to alter some of the bitterness and hateful feelings. When these intense emotions build, they act just as the intense emotion of love did initially. It became all-pervasive and literally took over your life. When one falls out of love and into hate, it also takes over and extends into all life areas. Not only does anger serve to cloud and confuse the minds of normally rational people, it also serves to get in the way of decision-making skills. For this reason, it is wise to go back to basics and start asking yourself questions about what your goals are in the situation in which you find yourself. Let us look carefully at how to evaluate the situation so that mistakes are not made.

When one looks at the issue of why a divorce is taking place, there are very important areas which should be carefully evaluated. By asking yourself the following questions, you may provide yourself with much needed rational thoughts and feelings. It will also give you the important opportunity to put the responsibility for the divorce where it belongs. The understanding that the break-up in the relationship is not the fault of only one of the partners and the awareness of your own responsibility is critical to good mental health. In a new age of exploring our own responsibility in relationships, answering these questions will allow for insight and personal growth.

1. What were my reasons for having wanted to marry this person?
2. What are the reasons why I want to end this marriage?
3. What part of the relationship went wrong in this marriage?
4. Did I have specific unmet expectations of my spouse?
5. Did my spouse have specific unmet expectations of me?
6. Will I be a happier person if I divorce?
7. What steps do I have to take to maintain sanity during this divorce?
8. Within the context of personal exploration, what must I do to attain more understanding and insight of myself and my relationships?
9. Is there any way to reconcile this relationship?
10. How will my next relationship be different? Similar?
11. Are there any other important aspects to consider?

There are several reasons why dealing with these questions becomes an important exercise. It is easy to get swept up in anger and make rash and harsh decisions that are not reality based. Oftentimes when an individual makes a decision to divorce, s/he feels that there is no way out and that it has to be done. However, there may be a way to save or reconstruct the relationship and this should be attempted unless it is an abusive situation. By stopping and checking our needs and motives, we can begin to make better decisions based more on fact and less on poor personality patterns. These issues should be fully explored. When issues are sidestepped and not investigated, they can easily take on a life of their own which is always highly destructive. When important issues are looked at, investigated, and not denied or avoided, answers and insights will be revealed so that prior poor patterns of behavior and poor choices do not have to be repeated. These insights will then enable you to view your divorce and the reasons for your actions in a new, saner and clearer light.

It is interesting to note that even though divorce is such a big step in a person's life, very few people actually spend enough time thinking about how it will feel. There are many intricacies in relationships which are usually taken for granted but which need to be explored in depth. If more people become aware of the serious emotional trauma they would be experiencing regarding the divorce, perhaps more people would try to rectify the relationship instead of running in the other direction. Not only are the emotions serious and deep but it then escalates when it is combined with the additional trauma of the legal aspects of divorce.

Emotional trauma always exists in divorces and most definitely affects the legal issues as well as how they are presented in court. These two aspects are not mutually exclusive and therefore cannot be separated away from each other. A healthy and smooth transition into being a single person from being a married person is not easy. For this reason, the psychological work has to take place. We strongly recommend that prior to filing the court documents for the dissolution, a full course of marital therapy takes place. This will help to raise consciousness about these questions and to help you deal effectively with the answers. By dealing with these questions within the concept of a new emotional awareness, your own awareness will blossom and this will benefit the process of transition.

It has been our experience that when a client consults with an attorney for the first time regarding dissolving a marriage, this client is always upset, hurt, angry and confused. This even takes place when an individual has thoroughly investigated the issues, gone through therapy, answered the questions satisfactorily, and is certain that a divorce is the correct action to pursue. There is always still considerable ambivalence along with anger, agitation, depression and many other feelings which make this a very painful experience. It is important to admit to oneself that divorce is an emotional and confusing time in each person's life. Although we are specifically focusing on the issue of divorce, similar emotional pain is also evident in the related issues of annulment and legal separation. Anything that interferes with long-term relationships has the ability to profoundly affect an individual's life.

The traumas of physical and emotional separations are the same. The feelings, emotions and legal aspects cannot be ignored. However, once again, by carefully investigating the issues involved in the previously discussed questions, new understanding can take place. The value of additional insight is also critical to the decision-making process. Insight is not always all-powerful. Insight does not necessarily do away with the sadness or disappointment or fear that most individuals experience. However, insight can certainly help to stop the feelings of being swallowed up by the emotions of the divorce. Insight will lead to a far clearer understanding of not only the reasons for the divorce, but also an understanding of the reasons and needs inherent in the marriage. Understanding and insight are extremely valuable tools for one to have in one's arseral of psychological skills.

With this additional insight, you can begin to see your divorce in a more global and more realistic manner. The small problems in which people get so caught up usually take a back seat to the bigger picture. When this negative process of nit-picking takes place, it blocks out more reality-based and psychologically healthy options. Each of us has to be aware that there are usually a great number of options available so that one does not have to drown in the quicksand of revenge and anger. When we see that it is easier to move forward into the divorce and get it done as smoothly and as cleanly as possible, we can bypass the anger and the agitation.

Our problems are made more complex by the court system which can only be defined as adversarial. When one enters the courtroom, it is immediately very clear that the other side is 'the enemy', whether one wants this to happen or not. The attorneys are adversaries who have the specific job of getting all that they can get for their respective clients. This adversarial system is unfortunately designed to do nothing but pull both parties down into the mire. The current system of divorce purposefully pits you against your spouse, and at times, even your children. The attorneys are automatically pitted against each other and the judge is there to act as referee between them and make certain that they play by the rules. The judge filters the data and tries to come to agreements but the parties are forced into seeing themselves through the eyes of the attorney in a win or lose situation. In the State of California these hearings are always held in front of a Judge or Commissioner. In some other states there may be a jury to hear a divorce, custody, or visitation matter.

We will discuss a bit later the options of Mediation and Collaborative Approach to Divorce, both of which allow the parties to, essentially, opt out of the adversarial court process and have much more control over their own destinies and divorce. The lawyers who participate in these options are far more interested in allowing the wife and husband to settle their differences amicably, or at least cooperatively, so that money and time can be saved, along with minimizing the emotional trauma of divorce.

Looking at several actual case histories will give us some information concerning the different reasons that people offer when they have decided to divorce:

"All I ever seem to do is take care of kids, the house and my husband. I rarely have time for myself. He comes home at night, sits down in front of the television, opens a beer and waits for me to serve him dinner. I know that he works hard, but I get little or no help around this house. I have tried to explain this process to him but it falls on deaf ears. I can't take it anymore and I feel that my only solution is divorce. I am emotionally upset and very angry with him, and unhappy with my life. And, it doesn't look like it will get any better if I stay married to this guy."

"I am going through a rough time at work and I know that I am a little more anxious than usual. But, she just isn't there for me, always working or off with her friends. She just doesn't seem to care much about me anymore. We hardly talk about important things and our sex life is non-existent. It would be easier for me

to come home to a house without her and just not have to deal with what is going on. I have tried to talk with her but she never has the time or the desire to listen. I see no choice but to get a divorce and I think that she would be happy if I told her that I was moving out. I know I would!"

"I am going crazy just being a housewife, mother and cleaning lady. I gave up a promising and potentially lucrative career to get married and to have children. Now, we are in a routine where I take care of everything and he earns the money. I need to pay some attention to the other part of me that wants to be successful, competitive, and out there in the world. I have tried to explain but he does not understand why I would want to go to work. Counseling is no option if he has no insight, and I am getting more and more frustrated each day. This just isn't what I thought married life would be. I am going to get out and salvage the rest of my life!"

"I come home from working very hard and the house is dirty, the kids are running around out of control, dinner is never ready, and she is either on the phone with one of her gay friends, busy doing something or out taking some odd-ball class. I am tired of living like this and she doesn't care what I think at all. There are other women out there who will treat me differently than she does, so why should I stay in this marriage? I don't know what to do about the kids but something can be worked out. I just can't take her anymore, and I want a divorce."

"I have been married to this slug for thirty-two years and now, with the kids long-gone, this marriage is empty. All of a sudden I see my future passing before my eyes and I'll be damned if I am going to spend it with this no-talent bozo. I want to experience life, something he doesn't seem to want to do. I don't even like him or his flea-bitten recliner anymore and I am getting out of this marriage."

"S/He was so nice to me before we got married; considerate and kind. Now, s/he has changed so much. I am no servant or slave. I can't even get anyone to listen to me. I guess I need to *get a divorce to stop all the fighting. I am tired of trying to make it work by myself. I want to meet someone who really appreciates me."*

All of these statements come from real people involved in real divorce cases. They are true and accurate samples of reasons that we frequently hear. However, are they the real reasons why these people want to get divorced? These bad situations have usually existed over long periods of time. Because of this, many people simply accept their lot and they become habituated to the unhappiness. Often, some new incident will crop up and this tends to set off a major reaction. These over-reactions lead to feelings of desperation and the immediate idea of wanting to change your life through divorce. This idea sounds good considering the pressure that is being felt and it cooks for a while as the individual begins to look for an attorney to consult. By this time, so little attention has been paid to the issues of the marriage and there is so much resentment that has built up that the marriage most likely is so broken down that it can no longer be saved.

Over our many years of experience we have noted that there are some specific differences apparent in the behavior of men and women when they make the decision that divorce is the correct path to take. When a woman decides that the marriage is over and she has made the decision to opt for divorce, she usually follows through and it is usually over. She has legitimately attempted to get her husband's attention throughout the relationship and she probably has felt put-down, pushed aside and ignored. By the time she decides that divorce is what she wants, she feels that she has tried everything that can be tried and she has lost all of her positive feelings for him. She has attempted to make inroads and all of her creativity has been exhausted. It is interesting to see that inevitably when she tells him that the relationship is over, and he actually hears it, he registers hurt, rejection and surprise. When the message finally gets through, the husband finally begins to listen to his wife and he tries to get her to give him another chance to mend the relationship. He has little understanding of why she will not forgive and forget. He does not understand that he had many chances during the marriage that he ignored and he does not understand that things have deteriorated to the point where it is simply too late. Because the husband puts so much stress on the wife for additional chances, she has a harder time leaving. This builds the guilt factor and sometimes, because the guilt is so difficult to bear, the wife will relent and give the husband yet another chance. However, she really knows that she is simply putting off the final divorce solution because neither her heart nor her motivations are actually in the reconciliation process. When a couple like this comes for therapy, it is very obvious that the wife has made her decision and that she will prevail. Resentments continue, fights take place again, and the separation ensues leaving both parties even angrier and more agitated than they were initially. It is important to see that from a psychological standpoint, it is most likely that the marriage could have been salvaged and reconstructed if the parties had come earlier. At this point in the process, there is no motivation for learning new skills and techniques. If the spouses could have talked effectively and listened attentively much earlier in the marriage, they would have been able to come to some creative and positive resolutions.

Men often exhibit emotionally rigid or emotionally lazy behavior. They will frequently stay with a marriage even when they really do not want to be with this woman any longer. Their reasons may run the entire gamut of: not wanting the discomfort of being alone; feeling guilt with regard to not being able to actively parent the children anymore; not wanting to look bad in front of the family; and, not knowing how to do domestic chores. Because of these and many other reasons, they avoid making their decisions. We have noted that this process takes place even when the man is aware that his wife does not care much for him. Once again they simply get into long-term bad habits and perpetuate these styles. This continues until perhaps a specific upset takes place which moves the decision along or until so much feeling is lost that they are barely related.

Many mental health professionals have agreed over the years that the manner in which women are parented generally helps them to become more aware of their deeper feelings than men. In addition, while many men find it painful to discuss feelings, women enjoy expressing, exposing and discussing these feelings. They confide in their friends, relatives, hairdressers, and their therapists. Men are parented in such a way that they grow with the general style that makes them seem to be less aware and less willing to share feelings. Some say that this may be a right brain or left brain function which is very specific to the sexes. Others attribute these styles to the societal growth patterns and the gender identified norms that we have accepted. Men are trained more toward non-verbal action or performance orientation rather than feeling awareness, while women are trained more to understand and discuss feelings.

Strong and deep relationships can frequently unleash feelings and emotions that feel foreign and strange in both men and women. These emotions can be positive such as intense feelings of love and joy that have never been experienced. They can also be equally negative feelings of anger and disappointment or the entire mid spectrum of feelings such as vulnerability, abandonment and jealousy. However, when the relationship deteriorates to the point where divorce becomes the most attractive option, it is the negative emotions that are experienced primarily. In addition, the spouse who wants the divorce may also have discovered newfound feelings of freedom and life. These specific feelings arise from the knowledge that the emotional suffocation within the repressed relationship is about to come to an end.

When we read the earlier classic examples of what people usually say concerning their reasons for divorce, it is clear that many of the reasons given can be relatively superficial. Although superficial, they are also believable, and they are also true. They are also very obviously able to be fixed. The complainer does not see this at all and is willing to let go of a very significant relationship, often over the smallest issue. However, research has demonstrated that underlying each complaint we can find deeper emotions as well as problems which may be rooted in long term personality or relationship difficulties. These problems may certainly have existed even prior to marriage. The intensity of a marital relationship can stimulate these difficulties and bring out the worst side of an individual. The need for divorce can bring deeper feelings to one's consciousness which were not known but were there even during the happy times. This can include feelings of low self-worth, jealousy, rejection, anger, fear, and chronic hurt. These negative aspects of personality may exist in the individuals as part of their pre-marriage make-up and general personality package. The breakdown of the marital relationship is at the same time a function of these problems and also brings these problems to the surface so that they are felt, exposed and have to be re-worked all over again.

The negative feelings which come up at the time of the divorce require examination. These are the feelings which underlie the need for divorce and support these reasons even if they appear as arbitrary. By carefully examining these feelings in a professional and detached manner, one can develop a better picture of self, a clearer understanding of why the marriage took place initially, and why the marriage is currently threatened by divorce. This is one of the modern challenges we face. The process of learning to grow and expand oneself through personal investigation and the taking of responsibility for one's actions is core to future growth and self-development.

Let us critically examine the circumstance of Frieda and David. Frieda is a young, attractive woman who was emotionally abused by her parents throughout her childhood. As a result of this negative system, she grew up being excessively careful and over-protective of her emotions. She had extreme difficulty allowing others to be close to her on any level of intimacy, and she especially avoided any depth of emotional intimacy with men at all costs. Since her parents were never supportive of her identity and they produced a great deal of ongoing insecurity in Frieda, she was consistently attracted to men who could give her a sense of physical and financial security. Because of this personality dynamic, Frieda married David. David is a pleasant, ordinary man with a good job, a good record of motivation, a conservative outlook on life and no experience at all with closeness. He is bland, not flashy, and very predictable in his behavior. Frieda felt that she could count on David for anything and that he would be loyal, true and not make excessive demands on her for intimacy. She knew that if David said that he would be somewhere at a specific time to do a specific thing, you could set your watch by him and confidently bet the farm that it would take place exactly as he stated it would. He was highly involved with his work, and very dedicated to his company, his boss and his family. Because of David's work drive, he did not demand much from Frieda in the emotional domain. This was very comfortable for Frieda. It allowed her to continue to protect her emotions, and helped her not to be intimate with David. As a famous police detective would say, "These are the facts and nothing but the facts". Based on this set of facts we can predict that one of two alternative endings will take place.

In the first circumstance, David eventually puts less emphasis on his work and turns to Frieda for his own security within the relationship. When he comes to the realization that Frieda actually has very little to offer him on an emotional level, David becomes excessively angry, feels that he has been defrauded and then he gets bored in the marriage. After a reasonable period of time where he tries to elicit feelings from Frieda, David gives up and lets his wife know that he wants a divorce. Frieda then becomes very angry, hurt, and keeps asking David why he is doing this. David honestly lists several good reasons for arriving at the difficult decision to dissolve the marriage. At this point, Frieda becomes highly defensive, very bitter, retreats into denial, and she then turns the tables and tries to blame David for everything. David, of course, does carry blame as well. His personality structure allowed him to be a loner and not require a great deal of closeness. Frieda's distance worked well for him for a long period of time. The actual divorce involved much blame, anger, continued bitterness and, of course, a great deal of money. Everyone loses!

Frieda could have seen this divorce issue differently. If she had looked at her own feelings early in the struggle rather than immediately placing blame, externalizing and projecting feelings onto David, it would have been helpful. If Frieda had accepted the challenge of self responsibility and had been able to carefully look at the reasons for her feelings of hurt, anger, and fear, she would have come face to face with her history. She would have gained insight into her personality structure and recognized the actual reasons why she married David. She would then be able to put the marriage and divorce in more proper perspective as she examined the answers to the questions we have posed. With this insight, she might have chosen to seek out professional mental health counseling to further investigate all of the patterns in the relationship which she brings, and, of course, those which David brings as well. Understanding the roles of the two parties in this marriage, and the manner in which their personality variables intertwined is critical and always goes far in resolving their problems. It is possible with this therapeutic approach, that the parties could have achieved necessary insights and learning which would have helped the marriage to sustain itself.

In this example, Frieda's new learning and insight would show her that she married a man who promised her security and who would not readily demand intimacy from her. She would come to see and understand the relationship between these needs as an adult, and her emotionally abusive childhood. By using this life event in as positive a manner as possible, Frieda would now be able to confront her fears, learn more about herself, and therefore not have to repeat this dysfunctional pattern with another man.

In the second alternative to the Frieda and David story, we see the possibility of an interesting serendipitous event. Frieda has a good friend named Lisa who tells her that she is attending a psychological seminar on relationships. Lisa tells Frieda that she has always felt close but she also has felt that Frieda has been afraid of closeness. She wants Frieda to go with her and she offers to make it a day together. Knowing Frieda, we can easily see that she would not want to attend because she tries to keep herself psychologically distant, bland, benign and unsophisticated. It is easier to be dumb about things than *it is to make changes. Therefore, why complicate one's life with self-knowledge? Her friend is insistent and Lisa prevails over a doubting and reluctant Frieda. They attend the workshop about adults who were emotionally abused as children.*

Frieda has a breakthrough experience and begins to remember her striking childhood anxieties. She feels hurt, angry, confused and, with Lisa's help, she recognizes that she can no longer function well unless she seeks out professional therapeutic help. She talks to the therapist who led the workshop and he agrees to take her on as an individual patient. After just a few very specific sessions, she starts becoming aware of some of her behavior and personality patterns. She realizes the dynamics of her marriage to David and why their distant relationship has not been very fulfilling for either of them. She begins to understand the issues around the central core of their relationship which was her need for a man who would provide security and not require much intimacy. She now has a renewal experience and wants to conquer these fears so that she can be a close, intimate and caring person with the man she loves. She explains this to David and offers him the opportunity to enter into conjoint therapy. Initially, David declines hoping that these struggles she describes will all pass and he will not be bothered further. With continued pressure from Frieda, David eventually relents and they work on their needs and their relationship. However, it is soon apparent that David and Frieda both have a great deal to learn and much psychological 'work' and growth ahead of them. In addition, it also becomes obvious to them that they cannot meet each other's needs and that they require different people in their lives.

Based on the therapy that Frieda has received, she sees that one of the life changes she must make if she is to grow emotionally is to dissolve her marriage to David. This is, of course, enormously painful to her. She is especially upset because she feels that David was not responsive initially when she offered him the chance to deal with their problems in conjoint therapy. Therefore, she is convinced that David has done absolutely nothing to give the marriage the opportunity to grow and have a future. The divorce is imminent, highly therapeutic for Frieda, but bitter. In this scenario, Frieda has taken on the modern approach of accepting the challenge of personal responsibility and expansion, while David continued to utilize the denial process until it was too late to save the relationship. If David remains mired in his position, he gives Frieda no choices at all except to follow through with the dissolution.

The story of Frieda and David is an excellent example of what can take place by looking at the needs, feelings and the emotions that underlie the expressed reasons both for marriage and divorce. You can put your divorce in excellent perspective by examining these feelings. This process will also permit you to see your own difficulties and stop externalizing all blame onto a spouse or others. This process is by no means an easy one. Self-discoveries and insight can be very painful to achieve, and even more painful if they lead to the divorce.

However, this process can also be highly advantageous and could lead to keeping the marriage going in a healthy and satisfying manner. If both partners are willing to open themselves to scrutiny and accept the challenge of helping themselves and their partner, it could lead to a most fulfilling situation. If the therapeutic process should dictate that the best alternative is divorce court, then the work in therapy pays off in other ways. Subsequent relationships will reap the benefits of the insights learned and experienced from the failed marriage. The pain of self-discovery is not always a happy process. However, it pays off in the future as it has the capacity to insure a positive result, better mental health, and future happiness. This can also help to change the tone of the divorce. Self-discovery aids in toning down the angers and reducing the battles. Of course, this does not mean that in a divorce each party should not try to get the best in custody/visitation agreements, financial support or division of property and debts. However, with newfound insights and perspective on the real issues and feelings, the insignificant fights can be put aside. The Popeye Magnet stops being the important icon when we become more genuine as people. When this happens, we learn the capacity to achieve a higher respect for others, even those we are divorcing. We can then learn to be more open, forgiving and less punitive. We can learn more awareness and take the time to thoroughly examine important feelings which can only help lead us to a better understanding of ourselves and our relationship.

Vengeance is often a driving force even though it is always negative. People who experience excessive anger and hurt blame their spouse for everything and use their need for revenge to escalate the hostilities. These types of clients are not at all interested in the 'why's' and 'how's'. Instead, they only want to assign blame and create excessive court battles that they can discuss for years to come. They obsess on the outcomes, no matter whether they are positive or negative, and they delight in boring everyone they know with the minutest of details. These are the clients who make it possible for attorneys, psychologists and other experts to buy expensive homes and cars and to send their children to fine colleges.

Throughout this book you will learn that all divorces, no matter how easy or officially simple they may be, are emotionally painful and very difficult. As an active participant in a divorce, you can now see the tremendous importance and the effects of the relationship between your emotional state at the time of the break-up and the activities which take place in divorce court. Even if your spouse should consciously decide that s/he wants to initiate the World War III game complete with heavy artillery, you still have the ability and capacity to approach the divorce circumstance with a much healthier and constructive attitude. No matter how difficult the divorce may become, it is important for you to have a clear and competent attitudinal set so that you do not plunge into the abyss of the warring trap. By attaining this healthier and more reality-based attitude, you will be able to make things go faster, smoother, and easier than if you too wanted to disembowel your spouse. By not buying into and experiencing this debilitating anger and hostility we can find a truly kinder and gentler way to live through this most difficult time in your life.

Ralph's story is a very good illustration of the complexity of divorce issues. Ralph was shocked when his wife of many years told him that she wanted to move out of the family home and be on her own. Ralph's work and his wife were his entire life. He had no idea in the world that there were major problems of this magnitude. Ralph thought that he had a good marriage and that he was experiencing everything worthwhile that life had to offer. Ralph became quite depressed and these feelings of misery and sadness continued for several months even after his wife left the home. Ralph then wisely decides to consult with a therapist who has a specific relationship-orientation in his treatment. After a few months of weekly treatment and before the actual divorce was to be filed, Ralph began to examine the reasons for his marriage and the reasons for his divorce. He realized that one of the driving forces in his personality structure was that he was fearful of being alone. Therefore, he began to understand that he spent all of his time doing things for his wife, not as a demonstration of love, but as a way of getting her approval. His outside interests waned until they finally disappeared. Through his newfound therapy, he started to achieve healthy, dynamic insights. Ralph saw that he and his wife were not as close or intimate as he once believed that they were. He saw that his marriage was really not supplying either himself or his wife with the kind of satisfaction and comfort that they both would have wanted. He realized how much he had been giving and how little he had been asking or receiving. By gaining this awareness of the underlying emotions and feelings, Ralph made many discoveries about himself and about his needs as a person. He came to the correct reality that because he was afraid of being rejected and left to be alone, he never spoke up and therefore sacrificed his individuality. His bitterness dissipated as he understood the import of his own role in the break-up. When he stopped placing all of the blame on his wife, Ralph began to experience feelings of relief, happiness and all-around better mental health. As a result, Ralph had no desire to make the divorce become such a difficult experience for his wife. He was now certain that his next relationship would be a more complete, more caring and healthier one.

Sally, another client, offers a case history which clearly demonstrates another aspect of the relationship between insight-oriented psychotherapy and the divorcing process. Sally was tired of her marriage and she was aware that the relationship had not been working for quite some time. She had thought seriously of leaving her husband and starting a new life. She ran down her checklist of issues and she felt certain that this was a good time to make the move. The children were all in high school and she knew that custody would not be an issue. They did have considerable property to divide but Sally had educated herself with regard to financial matters and so she felt that she could hold her own in this aspect. Sally was very bitter about having had to endure a marriage where she viewed herself as the good, caring, intelligent person while she viewed her husband as the angry, selfish and stupid person. She had decided to use this divorce to give her husband a strong taste of how miserable he had 'made' her during those long years of unhappiness. Sally decided out of her anger that she would make the divorce very tough and that she would refuse to make any settlements without a full-blown court hearing and a judge's decision. She was dedicated and her anger and agitation was clearly responsible for doing exactly what she had promised herself, forcing the case into court over and over again. When counseling was suggested to her, first by her attorney, and then the court mediator, and, finally, the judge, Sally became even angrier. "Why should I be the one to see a counselor when this whole thing is Bill's fault?" she protested. She was not interested in the excellent and reasonable offers made by her husband with regard to the property settlement. As a result, both parties paid for a long and completely unnecessary expensive court battle. This is a very good real-life example of what can happen when an individual's judgment is clouded because s/he has not looked into the underlying reasons for the marriage and the divorce. In the future, Sally will undoubtedly find herself in another relationship offering very little personal satisfaction because she did not take this valuable opportunity to learn more about her own psychology.

We have noted that many of the agitated people that we have encountered over the years in our psychological and legal practices have gone through two, three or more divorces. It is often more than astounding to see that in so many of these cases, each of the ex-spouses invariably turns out to be an almost exact carbon copy of the original spouse. The similarities, not only physical, but also psychological, are obvious and striking to everyone. In fact we even had one client who married two women with the same name. This is not an atypical circumstance. Each of us has had a divorced friend who has produced a new soon-to-be spouse and, of course, the friend has loudly announced that s/he has finally found the "perfect mate" who embodies all of the qualities that were missing in the ex-spouse. Why does this happen? Why are mistakes made over and over again? Why is it that we are often so blind to the fact that this new mate looks, sounds and acts just like the previous mate? The answer is quite simple since it is apparent that the friend has learned nothing from the agonies of the prior relationship, from the intricate couple dynamics and from the uncomfortable divorce. The old, disturbed patterns are being unconsciously reproduced and played out over and over again in the naïve unconscious hope that this time, with this new person, perhaps everything will turn out right. They will continue to be played out until something forces some insight.

Just as a good friend does not ever let a friend drive drunk, a good friend also should not allow a friend to marry blind. This does not mean that each of us should suddenly become a professional psychologist to everyone that s/he knows, or to continuously confront each and every friend and relative. Instead, a little kind caring and friendly advice very tactfully presented at just the right time could literally save a psychological life.

All of these case histories show us the interesting parameters of life as it involves the divorce court. Obviously, there are many different choices that can be made and many different avenues and approaches that can be taken. We do know that the best approach involves the application of positive action, positive thinking and positive emotional health. If you find yourself locked into a divorce, even if you are not the partner initiating the action, ask yourself how this divorce can lead you to experience personal growth. By extending the focus from the present to the future and trying not to be caught up in the emotions of the break-up, a very different perspective can be developed. Begin to think about taking care of your own needs. If you have attempted reconciliation, made serious efforts, and it has failed, then perhaps you have to accept that the divorce is going to happen, no matter what you want. Therefore, it is completely psychologically unproductive and even counterproductive to spend all of your energy ruminating, brooding, and fighting the process. That effort can best serve you if the energy is placed in making good things happen in your life. Be aware that in fact, you really do not want to be married to someone who does not want to be married to you. This is now the time to become involved in a healthy psychotherapy process to look at how to make your own future more fulfilling!

The issue of bitterness in divorces is legend. In the courtroom we see couples who began their lives together caring for and loving each other. Now, they are in the throes of anger and they are sitting apart from each other, never looking at each other and legally slugging it out. Some of the bitterest of divorces have taken place when one partner is determined to end the relationship while the other cannot accept the inevitable and believe that the marriage is truly over. In this circumstance, the person who wants to keep it together at all costs, may do completely inappropriate actions out of his/her emotional blindness. Some believe that if they make it more bitter and more miserable, the spouse will give up and come back to the marriage. For these people it seems more important to control, to keep the relationship together than it is for them to be psychologically healthy people. Being a slave to another person or trying to psychologically beat the other person into submission in hopes of maintaining a marriage is completely inappropriate and always doomed to failure.

All of the examples that have been offered should allow you to look at divorce as a reality. Even if you want the existing marriage to stay together, you can realize that there are situations in which one has no control. If this occurs, then it is critical to examine why you are having so much difficulty with the process of letting go of the marriage. When a divorce is actually happening, the signal is clear that this was not a very good marriage for at least one of the partners. If this is the case, then the relationship probably has not been good for either person. For some, it is difficult to look at the circumstances accurately because of the fear of being without a relationship with a significant person. This fear can often be excessively strong and even overwhelming since we are all basically social beings. This need has been known to blind individuals to everything but keeping things together at any cost. This is most definitely a serious mistake. This is the type of person who certainly could benefit from seeking out professional mental health therapeutic assistance. This is the person, and it may be you, who needs to learn new skills in coping with and understanding the divorce. This person also has to learn to utilize more critical thinking to identify the spouse's needs and learn to view the spouse in a more objective and less subjective light.

The purpose of this discussion is to open your 'psychological eyes'. In this manner you will be alerted to the need to see your divorce from a new, a different, and a definitely healthier perspective. It is important to keep in mind that a protracted, angry and hostile divorce will negatively affect all other aspects of your life. Children, family, friends, work, emotions, finances and future happiness for all considered are affected.

It is difficult to focus on becoming fulfilled during and after the divorce transition if you are caught up in an angry protracted battle. Many times these battles continue past the divorce because parents fight over children. However, a healthy and psychologically sophisticated attitude will assist you with a much better perspective on relationships, marriage and divorce. It is this perspective which views relationships in the context of your whole life and not just in the narrow context of the divorce which can lead you out of the trauma and into the light. In this manner, an individual can learn to focus on happiness in the future and begin today to involve him/herself in all those activities which are necessary to insure that it will come about.

CHAPTER 2
TALKING TO YOUR SPOUSE ABOUT DIVORCE

When a divorce is about to occur, for whatever reason, it is safe to assume that a great deal of acrimony and anxiety has preceded the decision. In the history of the world, it has probably never happened that a married couple has agreed on the same day that they will divorce, smile sweetly at each other, shake hands and go their separate ways. This is not what one would expect in real life. A rational discussion between two people regarding the fact that one or both want a divorce is rare. When only one wants the divorce the other is not going to be cooperative because that person simply has not reached the same point. Talking to your spouse about divorce is going to be a difficult and painful process. However, it can be done and should always be attempted. Certainly it is especially difficult if your spouse has no insight into the problems and does not wish to divorce. The author has seen many people in the process of divorce who were completely dumbfounded and terribly hurt because they were in denial and never had a clue that there was anything wrong. Ideally, the first part of the talking process has to be a brief education presented in a caring manner so that your spouse has some understanding of the depth of your problems. This will lend some insight into the seriousness of the issue. Dealing with the potential unlimited number of responses in the universe, it is very threatening to imagine what your angry or hostile spouse will say or how s/he may act. However, no matter how threatening this potential may be, the only healthy way to handle this important issue is to deal with it head-on and face it squarely. When one does discuss the prospect of divorce honestly, it will inevitably result in a feeling of ease and freedom. This is the first step toward ending the relationship that has now been hurtful, negative, anxiety producing and non-productive.

If you are a seriously abused spouse, then the rules change and we address that toward the end of this chapter.

Before talking to your spouse about divorce, it is expected that a great deal of time and psychological reflection has been spent dealing with the points made in the previous chapter. Knowing that this is not a decision which should be taken lightly, you will best be served by spending the time and doing the agonizing work of dealing with the reasons why you want your marriage to be over. This can be done in self-introspection and spending useful time in a solitary contemplative fashion. The depth of this decision is so critical that it is strongly recommended that a mental health professional be consulted so that positive insights and enlightenment can be fostered. If one makes this dedicated search with seriousness and care, awareness can flood in to fill the void and clear up misunderstandings. One can begin to recognize that anger and bitterness and depression are completely unproductive and that attempting to hurt your spouse or exacting revenge is not at all appropriate or productive.

These kinds of insights will result when one starts to take responsibility for his/her individual role in the marriage. It is never only the other person's fault. It is a responsibility which must be shared by two people. When these insights are reached, it will free up both parties so that they may begin to look toward a new and exciting future. This then permits both spouses to see the numerous possibilities which are available to them. This has the benefit of potentially promoting happiness and stopping the feelings of being stuck in an angry and unpleasant relationship. This type of behavior accepts the challenge of concentrating on personal growth and responsibility.

Most divorce discussions occur at the wrong time. When a married couple is in the midst of a bitter and hostile argument and one screams out, "I want a divorce" it has very little meaning. When this scenario takes place over and over, both parties begin to see that the statement has meaning and significance in their lives. When some insignificant disagreement escalates or when one of them feels that the ultimate breaking point has been reached, the argument becomes threatening or it dies and the problems are not resolved. This is not the time to tell your spouse that you want a divorce. When things are relatively quiet or tense but not hostile, this may be a better time to let your spouse know about your feelings. Very few people ever give this much thought because they are usually viewing their spouse with the object of seeking revenge for some real or imagined wrong, or at least the cause of their problems.

The object, of course, is to present the issue in a way that will be less hurtful. It is important to remember that the easier this is on your spouse, the easier it will also be on yourself. For this reason it is wise to have these discussions in the presence of a trained marriage (or divorce) counselor. The smoothest, most competent of divorces will inevitably be the ones which take place with an absolute minimum of anger and frustration and heat.

What can you do to keep as much of the anger, bitterness and frustration out of the divorce process? First, a private, personal, introspective investigation must take place. This must not be done quickly, but for as long as you require in order to become aware of the actual reasons for the lack of satisfaction in the marriage. This will enhance your perspective while at the same time it will also allow you to see your own responsibility and role in the disorders. This process gives rise to a most critical concept. Each of us always thinks that any problems we might have are always created outside of ourselves by other people. However, when the issues are seriously observed and investigated, it becomes very obvious that the old adage that "it takes two to tango" is actually true. These idioms are passed down through generations in our culture and we hear them as we grow up because they have been demonstrated to be absolute truisms. Utilizing a philosophy involving self-responsibility, we can see that when each of us understands that we share the guilt for the marriage break-up, then we can actually begin to work to drain off the anger and the frustration that we feel. This is a most important realization because it allows us to accept blame and not place all the blame on our spouse. In addition, this is the time to be aware of how potentially meaningful this other person will be throughout the remainder of your life. If there are children involved in the marriage, there is no doubt that you will have the continuing obligation to be communicating with your ex-spouse to deal with issues centered on future child growth and development. No matter how much you wish to avoid meetings, you can expect to come face to face with your ex-spouse at school functions, graduations, weddings, karate practice, baseball games, soccer, and other special occasions of all types. And children hate to be put in the middle of a battle of the parents. With this in mind, it becomes very clear that it is to your advantage to maintain a good working relationship with your ex-spouse for as long as possible. Rather than open up or inflict very deep wounds and wait for time to heal, the time to try and heal wounds is long before they get deep or begin to fester. Punitive desires will heighten the agitation, prolong the agony and not allow for a smooth, competent and cooperative divorce to take place.

    When one is absolutely confronted with the prospect of ending a marriage, there may be so much grief and frustration that very little time is spent productively. They also secretly think and plot as to how to get back at the ex-spouse for not being the fantasy marriage and sex partner that they had desired. Of course, these attitudes will interfere rather than help the individual make the adjustment and the necessary transition from being an unhappy married person to being a successful single person. The long-range results of these attitudes will always be disastrous. In order to avoid these negative consequences, each individual needs to spend time concentrating on all the options of both the negative and the potentially positive results when all is handled correctly. This thought process will present insights and help to keep the breaking-up-time freer from some of the negative feelings of anger and frustration.

The point at which you are going to actually let your spouse know that you have a strong and irreversible desire to divorce is a crucial moment in your relationship and in your life. Why is this so critical? Be aware that what you do at this point will be remembered forever. It will be right up on top of the list of horror with December 7, the assassinations of Dr. King and President Kennedy, and 9-11. Therefore, the manner in which you handle this challenge can set the tone for the future relationship with this person to whom you have been married. In many cases a couple may know each other all of their lives which makes it even more important and critical to realize that in some form, the relationship will continue forever. It is well worth thinking about other phases of your life in concert with your ex-spouse. In this manner you can both plan effectively for the future of the children. It is best for them to have a close and important ongoing relationship with both parents, not just with one parent.

The question of whether you would want to encourage a loving relationship between your children and your spouse, or whether you want to sabotage and spoil that relationship is an important one indeed. If you encouraged a loving relationship between the children and your ex-spouse while you were still married, what could have possibly changed which would alter this philosophical position? Very few people have the sense to recognize that when they attempt to keep the children from the ex-spouse or play courtroom games, they do not punish the ex-spouse, but instead, they actually punish the children. In addition, although they punish the children in the short run, they always wind up punishing themselves in the long haul. When the children get older so that they can see and understand what has really taken place between their parents, they will inevitably pay the offending parent back with rejection or specific acting-out behavior. Children become seriously confused and disturbed when they are used. When a parent encourages them to have a good relationship with the other parent and then suddenly stops doing this and does the opposite, the children learn that this is manipulation. This behavior confuses them and sometimes makes them not only angry but very literally disturbed. This behavior sends out multiple messages and makes no sense not only to the children, but it also makes no sense to an intelligent adult. This is the time to consider what the future working relationship will be with your ex-spouse as well as how you will set the stage for your children to grasp how people cooperate with each other.

Children always learn by incorporating and imitating the models of behavior that their parents offer them. Because of this, it is not at all unusual to see young boys with great disdain for their sisters, mother and female friends, because they imitate their father's negative attitudes toward their mother. It is also not unusual to see very young children talking about things such as child support and separate property disagreements of which they should know nothing. If you attempt to gain more self-respect by destroying your ex-spouse in the eyes of your children, you will be involved in a negative process which is mentally and psychologically unhealthy. We can absolutely guarantee that it will always, always backfire! If more people thought ahead and became more aware of this backfire potential, divorce would be a very easy, quick and uncomplicated process.

If there are no children in the marriage, then you may feel that many of the reasons cited for wanting to maintain a good relationship with your ex-spouse may disappear. Simply because there will be no ongoing relationship does not make the issue of human decency and courtesy moot. This is an individual with whom you have experienced a long and intimate relationship. Courtesy toward that person will undoubtedly repay you in the future with less hassle and aggravation. Practicing care and concern for others is a very healthy process. In addition, at this point, you still have no alternative but to discuss the issue of divorce with your ex-spouse and to work together so that you will both understand the best way to handle the problems. By not attempting to denigrate your spouse, you will significantly add, in a positive manner, to the complex process of making the transition from married person to single person, far easier and smoother.

Once there is recognition of the problems by both parties and it is clear that a divorce is forthcoming, the parties will be entering the legal system. The manner in which you handle the initial discussion of the separation and the divorce will have a direct relationship on the complexity and the difficulty of the upcoming legal questions. If the two parties are able to make a smooth transition from being together to being apart and accepting the separation, then most likely neither participant will want to intentionally inflict unnecessary or malicious pain on the other during the divorce action. If there is not a healthy discussion of the reasons for divorce, this initial phase of separation could also be fraught with anger, intense frustration, histrionics and agitation. If this happens, the stage is set for a difficult legal battle in which both participants use the courtroom and the legal system to vent their anger and frustration. It is not possible to control the manner in which the spouse responds but respect can allow the other spouse to save face and be calm rather than vindictive. Once you have made your decision to separate or divorce and once you begin to communicate this decision to your spouse, you will quickly see how this person accepts the information. Discussing the issues with an open attitude of non-blame and courtesy can most definitely save an enormous amount of aggravation, both psychological and legal. It is always worth taking some time to see things from the perspective of your spouse and having some empathy for him/her, whether or not you care for them any longer.

If you are clear as to why you were married and if you are clear as to why the marriage has not lived up to your expectations, then you will also be willing to take your share of the responsibility for its ending. Once this takes place, the discussion between both parties can be forthright and comfortable so long as the concept of blame is kept out of the conversation and not introduced. Neither spouse need blame the other nor be defensive toward each other. With the understanding that divorce, no matter how amicable, is a universally stressful situation, it is important to do everything possible to neutralize some of the inevitable emotionality. The object is not to create a war but to solve one. One wants to create an atmosphere between both parties which allows the opportunity to smoothly transition into separation. This is not done by being blind to one's own role in the marriage or by blaming the spouse for all the problems. Denial is an ugly mechanism and will always significantly interfere with any positive action which is attempted. When blame becomes the central focus of the issue, the discussion inevitably deteriorates into a screaming battle where neither party can be honest or caring because of the mutual threats.

When dealing with divorce issues, the question to ask yourself is, "Exactly what do I want to accomplish?" The decision to divorce a spouse carries with it large amounts of rejection and it embodies the entire emotional and psychological trauma that each of us fears. Within the human values and needs in our culture, the specific need to pair, to bond with another person, to depend on one another, to support and to give to another, is a primary need. We fear divorce because we feel that it represents our failure to achieve these primary goals. We are all embarrassed when we cannot maintain that ever-important relationship that our cultural mores insist on and require us to have. We sometimes place other people on a pedestal far above us and we always place the concept of the relationship on a pedestal. When this relationship does not hold and it breaks up, human beings typically go through a gut-wrenching and seriously painful process. Divorce encompasses more than emotions. It is a legal process and therefore, it ultimately ends up in court which is always adversarial. Rather than concede to the process and open a major battle, issues should be discussed and settled as early as possible. You do not want a judge who does not know you, your ex-spouse or your children to make decisions as to how, where, and with whom you will all live your lives. The time to anticipate the court issues is when you are ready to discuss divorce with your spouse. It is critical to remember that all of the court actions will be directly affected by this discussion.

The main idea inherent in changing the atmosphere from hurt and pain to progressive, positive, and valuable thinking involves the process of working together in a cooperative manner. It is not possible to always anticipate all the reactions your spouse will offer when you express your desire to end the marriage. You can take some of the responsibility by phrasing things in a non-combative fashion. You can work hard to convince your spouse that you want to work together in a respectful manner so that everything can be as smooth as possible. You should be ready to supply well thought-out creative compromises. You can offer resolution to problems rather than just stating the problems or blaming your spouse for the problems. In this manner your spouse will see that you want to work together to separate and resolve the issues with an air of positive and respectful thinking. The issues of money, property and children are highly emotionally charged and can result in terrible court struggles which often go on for years. The author has seen cases which come up monthly because the parties will take every opportunity to undercut each other and make life miserable. By working together, the parties can save their money so that they can educate their own children rather than the children of their attorneys or their psychology experts. When a person exposes his/her position and takes the risk of demonstrating honesty, openness and sincerity, it is possible to offer the other the opportunity to make this ending a less painful process. We hear many, many horror stories of persons who lie, hide money, and do all that they can to avoid their responsibilities. Unfortunately, this seems to be the current norm, and it is very responsible for keeping many attorneys and psychologists in full employment. We recommend strongly that the best approach is a direct, honest approach that will quickly convince the spouse that none of these devious activities will be undertaken. When all of the assets, properties, and the check registers, and the ledgers, and investments and expenses are open and above board, the divorce will go far smoother and trust will prevail. This may seem like the ultimate fantasy since we are dealing with an emotional situation where people usually now seem to dislike each other. However, it has been our experience that this open process most definitely can be accomplished. Not only can it be done, but it can also be done quite well. Trust is a very powerful factor and when it exists and is demonstrated, it can override a great deal of the hurt and anger.

It is possible of course that the honest and direct approach will not work with someone who is acting in an irrational manner. It is possible that your spouse will be so upset that s/he will not want anything to do with you, let alone want to work things out with you. Whatever happens, it is never appropriate to throw down the gauntlet and accept the obvious request to duel. Fighting is not what you want and it cannot help you to make your points clearer. Verbal or physical sparring or fighting is absolutely not a part of this equation and should never be accepted as a resolution of any problem. Even if one partner wants to fight and struggle, the fight does not exist if the other partner is able to remain calm, quiet, giving and understanding. The correct response is to back off until all tempers cool. Once this takes place, you may then want to continue to offer your spouse the opportunity to change thinking and actions and work cooperatively with you in this transition. Leave the door open to work together at all times. If your spouse remains angry but hires a reputable and competent attorney, then this attorney will counsel your spouse to work cooperatively. In addition, since you are the partner who wants the divorce, you have to understand that this is a new concept for your spouse. S/he may require more time to reflect on the issues, mull them over, and decide how to feel. Once this time is taken, the initial overture that was made for a peaceful process or working together cooperatively will seem more attractive. Each positive, honest and clear response you offer will increase the probability that a similar response will be forthcoming. Each positive, honest and clear response you offer will be effective in draining off the negative emotion from the legal struggles. During the active discussion of separation and divorce, excessive and very emotional over-reactions should be avoided. By being slightly detached from the emotion and as objective as possible, the issue will take on a clearer and healthier perspective. You have already thought these issues through while your spouse may be hearing them out loud for the first time. The surprises may be highly anxiety producing to your spouse and will take time to integrate and understand. Do not be surprised or overwhelmed if everything you present is not immediately accepted. It may require numerous discussions over a long period of time. The amount of effort you expend trying to create a cooperative atmosphere where compromise and new ideas are accepted is destined to pay off handsomely. With the correct approach, you will eventually elicit a positive response from your spouse. Some people mistakenly feel that because they choose not to carry on an active fight with their spouse, they will have to give in to the legal issues as well. This is not true and an air of cooperation will go a long way to smooth the court struggle.

There are steps which can be articulated, which, when followed, will enable the discussions to move further. Of course, the most important aspect is to be certain to have the discussions. Try to bring up the topic frequently and be certain that it is brought up in the right place, at the right time, and in the right manner. Be aware that you will need to handle these discussions with tact. You may have to temper your statements to fit the attitudes, styles and skills of your spouse. If you are dealing with an individual who may have a history of violence, or someone who has a history of drug or alcohol addiction, you may fare better by leaving the house and keeping your distance. Discussions with this type of spouse are better held in the office of a therapist or attorney or with a neutral friend or calm family member in attendance. You have to be aware that no discussion will be fruitful if the circumstances are not correct. You have to be the judge of the circumstance and open the discussion with your spouse when you have the maximum opportunity for acceptance and understanding. When these discussions do take place, make certain that they will be at a time and place when and where you will be least likely to be interrupted. Make sure that the children are asleep or not at home since they should not overhear or be a party to these negotiations. Compliment your spouse on the parts of the relationship that have been positive. Certainly it could not have been all bad and all relationships will have some funny and positive memories. The conversation should not be made up of solely negative and blaming statements. Indicate immediately your realization that you accept part of the responsibility for the failure of the relationship. Offer specific alternatives as to how the two of you can accept and make the transition into separation smoothly. Let feelings come and show your spouse that this is not a happy occasion. It is perfectly reasonable to reveal the fact that you are sad and uncomfortable about the break-up of the marriage. Ask your spouse for ideas and suggestions as to how s/he would like to handle things. Make certain that you are listening and accepting rather than being defensive. This is an opportunity for you to find out about the areas in the relationship for which you will take responsibility and of the things about you which your spouse has not liked or appreciated. Remember that this becomes one of your most important challenges. Since all agree that the current relationship is breaking up, there most likely has been a significant communication difficulty. Honest and effective communication can now be utilized since there is no longer anything to protect or defend. If both partners approach this situation with honesty, and treat each other with respect, the entire atmosphere will be changed. Since both you and your spouse do have positive and enjoyable memories as well as problems, it is helpful at these times to reminisce and to relive some of the old positive memories. This will certainly go a long way to create a more comfortable and friendlier atmosphere.

    The issues which will be brought out in court can be dealt with prior to asserting an all-out, full-blown, legal battle. These issues should be discussed with both parties and their attorneys in informal discussions. Many agreements can be made in these discussions. Judges very much enjoy ratifying any stipulations that the parties and attorneys can draft. This helps to manage the time in court and helps to cut down the acrimony. Even if the discussions get heated, they can continue as the parties, guided and assisted by their attorneys, move through the feelings of anger, disappointment and frustration. The smoother and faster the court activities, the more financial, psychological and emotional resources will be left. In addition, this means less stress for the children and therefore fewer problems with their acting-out behavior during and after the divorce. With the attitude of cooperation everyone will be saved many tears and much anxiety which will help them to be able to make giant forward moves in their new lives.

    Taking the time and expending the energy to handle the

dissolution of your marriage in a competent, rational and appropriate manner is very difficult. It is far easier to give in to the destructive feelings, rant, rave and grab. Often people feel that they are not able to face their spouse with what they truly want to say. They also know that the other party will have many negative things to say back and they are afraid to hear anything which they know will produce discomfort. This process of talking with your spouse requires much courage. It will undoubtedly cause you to see that you may not have been quite as good a husband or wife as perhaps you thought you were. However, you can be sure that the ultimate benefits of opening up all of the information to the sunlight will far outweigh the liabilities. The courtroom battles are designed to produce only losers. Therefore, it is far better to deal with it in the living room or meeting room thoroughly than it is to deal with it in the courtroom. The specific goal you seek is enlightening yourself, enlightening your spouse and making as smooth a transition as possible. This will temper the harshness and anxiety of the divorce and produce two adult fully-functioning persons. This reduces the stress on all concerned and creates a win-win proposition to replace the original lose-lose status.

Sharon and Jim had been married for nine years and had three children, ages seven, five and three. They had never had a distinctly happy time through the length of their entire marriage. Both had been exposed to negative and hostile abusive childhood circumstances and neither seemed to know how to have happy relationships. Since they were both protecting their feelings and being very cautious, there was little intimacy between them and even less trust. They had married at a young age in order to feel like adults, leave their parental homes and change their lives. Jim prided himself on his ability to be a hard worker. It was clear that he very much enjoyed the role of worker-provider-father of the family. Sharon stayed at home with the children in a traditional fashion and rarely worked outside the home. They both performed their traditional roles, Jim as worker and Sharon as homemaker and childcare specialist. The more hours Jim worked and the more money he was able to make, the more Jim enjoyed life. Since he was happy with his role and since he believed that this was what he was supposed to do, Jim was completely unaware of everything else. He was unaware of the fact that there were serious marital difficulties brewing in his relationship and that Sharon was starving for his attention. Although his role was highly satisfying to him, her role was only minimally satisfying to her. Sharon tried to telegraph her unhappiness but she never opened up and instead she utilized veiled, obtuse mechanisms, hoping to catch Jim's attention. Because of this amorphous approach, Jim was not receiving. Sharon, in her ever-present feeling of unhappiness, felt certain that something truly important was missing from her life. She became more and more introspective and she began to heavily involve herself in reading various self-help books. She then sought counseling from a therapist she had seen years before. She also spoke at length with her friends and family regarding the deficiencies she felt in her relationship with Jim.

Within a short period of time, it became evident to Sharon that she had married Jim for security and not for love. In fact, she recognized that Jim was actually very much like her own father who had always been very abrupt and withholding of positive emotional expressions. She noted that unlike her father, Jim was able to be quite affectionate with the children, but he was not affectionate toward Sharon. She also began to achieve insights regarding her own behavior patterns and she decided that the time had come to make changes. She had profound understandings as to who she was and what she now desired for her life, specifically with regard to her relationship with Jim. Time and again Sharon attempted to speak to Jim about the patterns she saw but he was simply not interested or not sophisticated enough to analyze their interactions. He refused to go with her for the conjoint marital counseling recommended by her therapist. In his stubbornness and stupidity, Jim offered Sharon no workable alternatives. Sharon realized that the only alternative open to her was to free herself of this relationship. She knew that this must be done if she was ever to be able to achieve happiness with a man in the future.

Sharon spoke intensely with her counselor and continued to study her psychological self-help books in preparation for speaking seriously with Jim concerning her desire to divorce. She spent time thinking about the style in which they related to each other and she spent time with paper and pencil outlining her desired roles in the family. She wanted to have a smooth transition in order to hurt the children as little as possible. She also did not want to hurt Jim any more than necessary. Sharon chose a good time to speak with Jim. She knew that he would become upset, and she was correct. As she carefully and thoroughly described her needs and told him her plans he demonstrated that he was very hurt and angry. His intense and somewhat explosive emotional reaction was very upsetting to both of them as he finally stood up straight and bolted from the room yelling out that he was not interested in divorce. He had no understanding of the situation, would not listen to her, and therefore, he could not comprehend her reasoning. He returned to the conversation a few minutes later but, as expected, he was not very productive. When he returned, he kept asking Sharon over and over if it would not be possible for them to try and work things out so that they could stay together. However, even while he was saying that he would work with Sharon, Jim still stubbornly held fast and directly indicated that they did not require the services of a marriage counselor. He was a traditionalist and proud of his position. Therefore, he felt that he would be embarrassed to go for marriage counseling. Jim said that it was not manly to share your problems with strangers. Even though Sharon had already decided that she did not have any interest in trying again with Jim, this cemented in her position. She felt that she had tried for many years and that there was no payoff to continue the struggle. She had threatened Jim with separation but, once again, he had never heard her. Sharon was upset that she had not been true to herself because she had never followed *through. Now she was ready. Sharon was telling herself that she was tired and that she wanted this marriage to be over. Through the process of her therapeutic self-examination, she had decided that Jim was not the man to whom she wanted to be married for the remainder of her life.*

Sharon remained as detached as she could throughout her discussions with Jim. She did not want to become a part of his anger and hysteria and she did not want to further inflame the circumstance any more than it already had been. She was very willing to take the responsibility for her own faults in the marriage and she explained honestly to Jim why she needed the divorce. She encouraged Jim to spend as much time with the children as he wanted so that they could continue to have an effective and cooperative co-parenting relationship. She indicated to him constantly, in the spirit of cooperation, that there would be no difficulty with the distribution and the division of their real property. She told Jim that she was not interested in a fierce court battle and this made Jim calmer. Sharon suggested that they establish a principle of fairness and respect in the service of the best interests of the children. This allowed Jim to be calmer and to save face in this circumstance.

Sharon's progressive and healthy attitudes allowed them and their attorneys to minimize the court encounters. Jim's feelings of hurt and anger interfered and this made the separation difficult. However, they had reality-based groundrules and a positive orientation due to Sharon's careful approach and calm demeanor. She clearly informed Jim that she expected him to treat her fairly and equally. She offered that she would do the same in return as no matter what the issue, she was determined to treat him in this manner. She modeled this behavior consistently until Jim and his attorney believed her. When Jim would get angry and threaten Sharon with taking the children and the money and all the property, Sharon simply did not react. She calmly indicated to Jim that she completely understood his feelings. Sharon had consulted with her attorney and she knew that Jim could not follow through with his threats. This gave her reassurance and helped her to remain calm and realistic. She understood that he unconsciously had a need to strike out at her because she had hurt him and ruined his life plan. Sharon understood, did not allow Jim to push her buttons with his yelling and threats, and continued to offer him as smooth a transition as possible. She also recognized that not reacting emotionally was not the same as giving up her legal rights. This consistent and competent attitude helped Jim to eventually calm down so that he could begin to deal with her in a rational and effective manner.

Sharon was careful not to involve herself in minor matters. Instead, she continued to concentrate and deal with the bigger picture. This permitted her not to get caught up in Jim's anger. Even though it was very difficult for Sharon not to react inappropriately as she felt she would like to, she persevered in order to make for an easier divorce. In order to be able to accomplish this and stick to her correct position, Sharon made it a point to spend a great deal of time reflecting on why she wanted this divorce as well as her role in the marriage. She shifted the main focus of her thinking from her desire to make Jim pay for her years of unhappiness in a bad marriage, to thinking about her future potential for happiness with someone else. Sharon also understood the very important need to maintain as good a relationship as possible between Jim and the children. She did not wish to damage this in any manner. Although it took some time, Jim did finally achieve insight and become aware of Sharon's honest motives and position. When he was convinced, he allowed himself to relax more and to let go of his fears of losing his children forever.

This example clearly illustrates that it is possible to lay down the foundations so that people, with courage and determination, can make a smooth transition from being married to being single. It is a difficult process but the long-term rewards are much greater than a bitter and miserable struggle through the bowels of the divorce court.

This area strongly suggests some important insights for

women. In the more traditional relationships, the husband deals with most of the control issues. He usually earns most of the money while the wife spends her time caring for the children and the home. This is unfortunate because, with the husband having the financial control in these relationships, the traditional husband is successfully able to intimidate the traditional wife. The wife becomes fearful of demonstrating any type of assertive behavior. When a break-up takes place, this intimidation factor makes all aspects of the divorce doubly difficult for the wife. She may not have a great deal of information concerning the family financial circumstance. In addition, she is certain that her husband will not be honest with her so she is frightened with regard to discussing finances with him. Knowing how important it is for him to maintain these controls, she may also be afraid that he will become emotionally abusive and/or physically violent if she presses the issue. This is especially true if the husband does not want the divorce. Because the wife feels that she may have no control in this situation she becomes afraid to make demands and requests even if they are reasonable. The husband can use his emotional and physical strength, his knowledge, his size and his intimidation skills to continue to control the funds. These ploys are designed to keep the wife dependent, to not allow her to grow emotionally, and to keep the husband in the 'top dog' position.

In this type of circumstance, a woman has no choice but to consult with a knowledgeable attorney and file for dissolution of the marriage. The attorney can advise her as to how best to freeze the assets of the community so that the husband cannot hide or squander them. The attorney can also obtain the appropriate and necessary restraining orders aimed at keeping the angry and potentially violent husband away. In this way, the wife can better control her fears of the possibility of any acting out taking place.

Once the attorney is involved and the couple has entered into the legal arena, the transition from being married to becoming a successful single person becomes even more difficult. In addition, it now becomes impossible for the wife to be able to honestly and openly discuss the marriage and divorce with her husband. It is important to note that there are times when it is appropriate to follow through with an attorney. When one spouse will absolutely not allow the opportunity to discuss the issues, then it is correct to begin to think of legally protecting self, children, property and other assets. However, it is critical that the individuals thoroughly test the situation prior to, and even after, making contact with the attorney. The reactions of the spouse will dictate just how involved you will have to become in the legal process. This should be discussed with your own attorney.

It is always surprising to us that in a large number of divorces, the wife is often nearly completely unaware of the couple's financial circumstance. We have seen this even in marriages where the wife was a successful businesswoman outside the home while she was totally in the dark inside the home.

Judy made an appointment with her attorney to discuss the steps necessary to procure a divorce. She was a high school administrator for a school district. She had been married over ten years to a successful businessman. The couple owned property, stocks, cars, assets, furniture, a boat, motorcycles, and bank accounts. However, when the attorney questioned Judy as to what her separate assets may have been, what her husband's separate assets were, what the couple or the community owned, and as to what all their debts were, she was embarrassed to admit that she knew very little. She had abdicated the entire responsibility for caring for their investments and assets to her husband. Judy remembered signing papers that were shoved in front of her but she never took much if any interest in the accounts they had. As a result of Judy's negligence, much time in her divorce was spent trying to determine all of the property that the couple had accumulated during their marriage. This consumes much of the attorney's time, thereby costing the client more money. In a circumstance such as this where the wife knows very little, combined with a secretive, angry and fearful husband, locating all of the assets can be all but impossible.

We have seen numerous cases where, because of a divorce, the woman has finally been forced to learn about the family finances and how to deal with them. She may never have written a check before, but suddenly she is thrust into a situation where she has to understand and manage property; deal with debts; credit lines; deeds of trust and other financial instruments. It is imperative to learn about all of these areas so that the client can assist the attorney to manage the economic part of the dissolution. It is unfortunate that culturally, our society tends to condone keeping women in the dark with regard to dealing with the family finances. The time is now to rectify this situation so that both spouses become equal partners with equal information, equal knowledge about their interests and equal input from their environment.

There have been cases where, because of physical mistreatment, the wife has had to take a long time before being able to loosen herself from her husband's psychological and physical grip. She may be afraid both for herself and for her children. This woman will be depending on receiving a great deal of emotional support both from family and friends before she will be able to make the final break. When the abused woman is able to find a supportive home to go to, it certainly becomes easier for her to make the move. In some instances, this woman may have no local family so that she is forced to make the move to a local battered woman's shelter. These shelters exist in larger cities and are usually supported by state or local funding. They were created especially for women and their children in this type of situation. The location of the shelter is kept confidential and the address is not even listed with the phone number so that abusive husbands are prohibited from finding their wives. To discover the ways to contact the shelter nearest to you, you may call the local Coalition Against Household Violence, the Office of the County District Attorney or the Office of the County Prosecutor. The personnel in these offices are always prepared to immediately assist the battered woman who wants to leave the abusive marital situation.

Sarah had been married for five years to her husband who had a history of drinking, losing self-control and exhibiting violence. When he would get upset, Sarah knew that she was in for a dose of yelling and screaming as well as possibly a physical beating. Sarah, embarrassed to be in this situation, never reported it or told anyone what was happening in her home. She did not wish to upset her husband because she felt that no matter what he did, she loved him. She foolishly believed, just as many battered women believe, that even though her husband hit her, he loved her too. After five years of abuse, Sarah began to have some insight into the fact that there must be a better way to live. She no longer wanted to be married to an abusive and battering alcoholic. She believed that she now deserved better and through therapy, she learned that she could survive without this man. After making numerous discrete inquiries, Sarah found that there was a battered woman's shelter nearby. One day, while her husband was at work, Sarah took some clothes and other belongings for herself and her daughter and they left for the shelter. At the shelter Sarah was assisted in contacting an attorney who then prepared the restraining orders, the divorce papers and arranged for the necessary hearings. The attorney contacted law enforcement officials to inform them of the restraining order situation and Sarah was able to extricate herself from a very bad marriage. Not long after this, her attorney was able to secure the home for Sarah and her daughter. This was done with the understanding that she and her daughter would be followed up by attending outpatient psychotherapy.

If you are an individual who falls in the category of an abused spouse, then you have no choice but to immediately call in an attorney who will file the papers for the necessary restraining orders and the divorce. It is not possible to have a reasonable and rational discussion with a spouse who has a history of violence and abuse, and you should not even try to do this. The typical pattern is that the abusing spouse will apologize very convincingly, swear not to do it again and then the behavior repeats in a few days or weeks. Instead, the important process to put into effect is to immediately break away and therefore not permit any of the negative abuse to continue. In addition to the dissolution of the marriage, and the filing of the restraining orders, criminal or civil charges can also be filed if the abusive behavior falls into a criminal pattern. It is unfortunately inherent in abused women that they wish to believe their abusers and they return to them numerous times. Sometimes this has to play itself out and the black eyes have to accumulate before the abused spouse is able to leave. It is critical for friends and family to attempt to intervene in this process since it may result in the saving of a human life. Most states have laws and well-defined penalties against spousal and child abuse for the protection of people in these situations. An individual who has a history of spousal abuse is not emotionally balanced. This person requires immediate psychological treatment, and, in many cases, incarceration is necessary. The desire to break away from this type of relationship is fairly universal. There are some individuals who have a disturbed psychotic, sado-masochistic problem where they feel that they require physical and mental abuse to live successfully. These people require abuse as if addicted, and they will thrive when beaten. However, this is very atypical. Most of the population of our culture knows at some level that abuse is a negative process. When the abused spouse realizes this, rises up and tells the abuser that this behavior will absolutely not be tolerated under any circumstances, then, and only then will life change. All people deserve respect and no one deserves violence!! One should never consciously place him/herself in a situation where an abusive husband or wife is able to do physical damage just because s/he knows that the relationship will be ending soon.

When an abuser comes into the courts, s/he is usually placed in a psycho-therapeutically-oriented diversion program. These programs can work. Although it takes a great deal of time and concentrated therapeutic effort, it is possible to make enormous changes in one's life. We have seen families reunited within the process of psychotherapy with excellent results. However, this is not something that a battered spouse should depend upon. It is not appropriate to place oneself in a physically and psychologically dangerous situation on a hunch or wish. Only after a great deal of time in therapy has passed with short visits should a battered spouse trust that change can be possible. This is extremely risky and it has been demonstrated that very few batterers actually change behavior enough so that reunification is possible. It is very necessary for both parties and their children to be part of a systematic therapeutic program where there are built-in safeguards for their physical protection. The battered spouse will have to very carefully and very realistically measure the batterer's behavior. We have been involved in numerous cases where our advice to the battered spouse was not to return to the batterer. However, most of the time this advice is not followed and the physical abuse circumstance repeats. In order for a battered spouse to survive, the dependence cycle must be broken.

CHAPTER 3
CHOOSING AN ATTORNEY

The process of selecting an appropriate and competent attorney is a difficult one indeed. The attorney you select must be a person who will counsel you and who you will trust to represent you correctly by representing your views, attitudes, and needs. At this point you have thought very seriously for a long time about the reasons why you want to get a divorce. You have inventoried your life and, in a rational manner, you have made your decision that your relationship with your spouse cannot be healed or changed appropriately. It is expected that you have made an honest attempt to discuss your needs and your desires with your spouse. By doing this you have attained some measure of success if only to let your spouse know of the seriousness of the circumstance and the depth of your feelings. You have now reached a definite point where you feel that you cannot negotiate effectively with your spouse. Therefore, you have reached the point where you must protect yourself, your rights and your property by seeking out professional legal representation.

Each attorney has a particular style, interest, specialty, and a particular way of looking at the process of divorce. Interview several attorneys before deciding with whom you feel the most comfortable. Many people forget that they are the ones who are doing the hiring of the attorney. Often people feel that the attorney is doing the interviewing and hiring the client. This is absolutely not the case, because the client must, at all times, be the ultimate decider on the issues of the case. It is all right to be highly selective and very particular since this person is so very important to your life at this time. In addition, remember that you will be paying the attorney for his/her services and you want your money to buy a good product.

Most people feel totally confused as to how to begin this difficult process of finding an attorney. There are any number of places where one can effectively begin and there are some simple steps which will lead to success. First, be fully aware that you must narrow down your search to attorneys who are qualified as family law specialists. No matter how much you like Uncle Harry's second cousin, and no matter how good he is at dog bite cases, he may be a disaster in the family law courtroom. You do not want a generalist, but instead, you want a specialist. Perhaps you have had some prior contact with a lawyer who either handles divorce matters or who can refer you to someone who has this expertise. Frequently, you will know others who have gone through divorces and these people should be consulted for referral to their attorney. An individual who has already been through a difficult emotional divorce will have gathered a great deal of basic knowledge with regard to the function of the attorney. Perhaps this person felt that his/her attorney was very good in the courtroom or perhaps this person saw another attorney who was more dynamic, knowledgeable and commanded more respect. This is a good way to get the names of competent attorneys since people who have seen them in the courtroom have evaluated them while they were literally under fire.

In each county there is a local Bar Association to which most attorneys in practice belong. It is wise to call and consult the secretary of the association who will have a book of members with their specialties and qualifications. In addition, if the Bar Association is large enough, there will be a sub-specialty group usually known as the Family Law Bar. If this is the case, you will have a list of well-trained and highly specialized attorneys to consult. Once you have looked through this list and culled out those attorneys with family law specialties, you can begin the process of interviewing. The idea is to find an attorney who not only has the necessary qualifications, but also one in whom you have confidence. In this way you will be able to feel that you can cooperate with this attorney, take advice and work well together. It is important to remember that you do not have to choose an attorney before you talk to one. Instead, it is perfectly reasonable for you to want to speak to the attorney first so that you can measure how this person fits into your criteria. Most people are naturally intimidated by lawyers so they are hesitant to confer with more than one. However, a divorce is a very serious and complex process and you must have an expert who will be able to plan the strategy and follow through. Therefore, you need not be intimidated and you need not choose anyone prior to having a conference.

Another effective way of selecting a qualified local divorce attorney is to go to the domestic court and become a court watcher. If you sit in court and watch the attorneys in action you will become familiar with the language and the procedures. By watching the attorneys in action, you will develop a far better feel for which of the attorneys can and cannot get things done. You can call the local county clerk who will direct you to the county courthouse and tell you which department calendars family matters and when these hearings are held. You will have no difficulty being an observer. It is only on very rare occasions that these hearings are closed or will take place mainly in the judge's chambers. These hearings usually take place in open court with the public invited. It is important to watch carefully so that you can learn to pick up small nuances of interaction in the courtroom. See which attorneys appear to have a good rapport with the judges and with other lawyers as well as with their clients. The attorney who is able to display confidence while appearing competent and comfortable in the courtroom can undoubtedly be called on to do a good job. The attorney who seems lost, confused, bumbling, unprepared, and shuffling papers should be avoided. Listen to how the attorneys form their questions.

Listen to how the attorneys deal with expert witnesses such as a psychologist or psychiatrist. You want an attorney who can ask the most intelligible questions so that your information can be effectively revealed to the judge. You want an attorney who forms questions well and does not get interrupted constantly by objections.

Court bailiffs spend all their time watching attorneys in action. They may not be hesitant to make specific referrals and they may be willing to give you names of attorneys. If the bailiff does not want to make a specific referral, chatting with him/her during a break can reveal much information regarding their observations of an attorney's competence. Court reporters can also be a wonderful source of information. Though they may be hard to catch and also hesitant to answer, they can still be asked. Court clerks are usually not a good source of information since they work for the judge and they are not really able to give out information concerning lawyers. While you are in court watching the action, you will find that there are specific breaks. During these breaks you might ask a few of the members of the divorcing couples if they are satisfied with their lawyers. This could lead to interesting responses and even more leads of attorneys to interview.

Finally, you will find that there is a small cadre of psychologists who do the psychological evaluations for custody. Successful, long time practicing psychologists with this specialty will have worked with all the attorneys in the county many times over. It would be wise to schedule an hour with a psychologist to review the strengths and weaknesses of the local family law attorneys.

Once you have accomplished all of this research we are suggesting, you need to put together a small list of the most competent attorneys. When you have put together this tentative list of attorneys, you can begin to narrow the choices to three or four names. Your homework will start to pay off when you call each of the attorneys and set up interview appointments. Be certain that you ask if you will be charged for the consultation. You will find that most experienced family law attorneys will likely charge for a consultation but it is worth it in the long run to pay this and hire a competent lawyer who is in sync with your views. If you choose to hire a particular lawyer you are consulting with, often the consultation fee can be included in the retainer payment.

    If your spouse precipitously serves divorce papers on you without discussion or warning and the time to respond is short, you may believe that the process of selecting an attorney has to be speeded up. A continuance of any court hearing can always be requested if you are not ready to deal with the issues. Judges are very solicitous of people appearing in pro per (unrepresented by an attorney) and s/he will certainly grant a continuance until you can find an appropriate attorney to represent you. If you feel too rushed, it is not wise to hire an attorney prior to researching the circumstances so that you can be certain the attorney will suit your needs. You have the right to go to court at the time of the hearing and tell the judge that you wish to be represented but that you have not had enough time to hire an attorney. Continuances for good cause are asked for and granted on a regular basis in every courtroom. Unless there are other extenuating circumstances, most judges will grant your reasonable request for a delay with no difficulty. This will give you a chance to breathe and make your search in a positive manner.

    In order to maximize your skills with regard to selecting an appropriate attorney, it is quite critical to prepare yourself for the initial consultation. When you are ready, you will be able to make the best use of your time as you actively determine whether this attorney should be the one to represent you in your divorce case. In fact, even after you choose your attorney, you should be careful to prepare thoroughly for each and every consultation session. Effective preparation will speed up the process and give the attorney all the data necessary to do the job correctly. In this way, your attorney will be able to understand your wishes, needs, rights and responsibilities so that s/he can accurately and competently represent you.

    It may seem very basic to say that you should know your case. However, we have seen many people without even the faintest clue as to what they want to say, what they want from the divorce, and what they have to support their case. They come without the paperwork that is critical for the attorney to have. In your divorce case, you will be dealing with a large number of basic questions. The major issues will usually revolve around custody of children, spousal support, child support, division of property, separate property rights, and outstanding debts. Bring with you to the meeting with your attorney the following information:

1. Date of marriage;
2. Separation date;
3. Prenuptial agreements;
4. Any agreements which would indicate separate property rights;
5. Information regarding the children: birth dates; current status regarding their dependence/independence;
6. A complete list of all property co-owned by you and your spouse;
7. A complete list of all property owned individually by you or your spouse prior to the marriage or during the marriage;
8. A complete list of all property co-owned by you or your spouse with another person or entity outside of the marriage;
9. The fair market values and appraisals of any and all real estate above, jewelry, other assets, as well as copies of deeds, closing documents and loan documents;
10. A list of all bank accounts held jointly with your spouse or individually by you or by your spouse along with account numbers and current dollar amounts;
11. A list of all investments, stocks, bonds, partnerships held jointly or individually;
12. A list of all credit cards, numbers, amounts owed;
13. A list of any other debts such as private loans from family members with the accurate amounts due and interest rates;
14. Pay stubs to show how much money you and your spouse earned within the last three years;
15. Joint or individual tax return, both state and federal, earned within the last three years.

As you look at the above list it may appear overwhelming and burdensome. It will be difficult to assemble all of this material and bring it to your lawyer's office, but this information will definitely be required at some time early during the divorce proceedings. Try not to feel overburdened, but instead, recognize that you help your own cause by helping your attorney to be well prepared. The earlier that you are able to get these items to your attorney, the more prepared the attorney will be and the better case you will have. The attorney will also be impressed by your effective preparation and willingness to help your own case which is very important if you wish to have a successful result.

It is also of great worth for you to spend some time thinking and to carefully prepare a list of questions that you will want to ask your attorney. Prior to the consultation you may be burning with questions and a strong need for information. If this is not written down in some orderly fashion it will inevitably get lost in the information of the meeting. When you remember the points later it does no good with regard to feeling informed. Do not be concerned even if you feel that your list of questions is excessively long. A good attorney will certainly understand your need not to be kept in the dark and your questions will be welcomed and answered. It will save time and money later so that you do not have to be calling the attorney continuously to ask things that you forgot. If you are organized, you will serve as a good model for the attorney who will appreciate your hard work and your desire to be helpful to your case. Attorneys have often confided that they are amazed at times regarding how little their clients want to know and also how long it sometimes takes for their clients to produce documents and papers that they require in order to properly represent them. If you feel that your attorney is getting upset or overly defensive about the questions you are asking, this is most likely not the attorney for you. Do not feel obligated to an attorney who is not doing the job well enough nor is communicating well with you and explaining procedures, court rulings and strategies.

When you are about to hire a divorce attorney, you must realize that this is going to be a demanding and close working relationship. Your attorney will be asking you to share important, and at times, intimate information. Therefore, you need to be very certain that this particular attorney will not hesitate to advise you and will represent you very specifically in the manner in which you want things to be done. This does not mean that you run the entire show or that the attorney runs the entire show. Instead, it means that you give guidance and direction to your attorney so that s/he will know how you want things to proceed. Be aware of the type of approach you want your attorney to take. Would you rather have an aggressive, assertive attorney or would you rather have a more contemplative and passive attorney? We have seen both positions work effectively. The dynamic three-piece-suit attorney who is super organized all the time and exudes confidence certainly can be effective. However, the old "I'm just an old country lawyer" lawyer also works very well. When you visit your attorney for the first time, the following questions should be asked:

1. How much of your law practice is devoted to divorce cases?
2. Do you have any specialty training or state certification as a family lawyer?
3. How long have you been involved specifically in the practice of family law?
4. How long have you been in this community?
5. Do you have a preference regarding representing men or women in divorce matters?
6. Do you ever represent children in divorce cases?
7. How accessible will you be to me regarding appointments?
8. What is your policy regarding returning phone calls?
9. What will you expect of me during this case?
10. Will you consult with me prior to making any agreements or doing anything of significance in this case?
11. Will you send me copies of all correspondence and court papers dealing with my case?
12. How will you keep me informed as to the progress and status of my case?
13. What is your general philosophy as to how to best handle and resolve divorce cases?
14. How do you feel about private evaluations and private mediations to resolve the conflicts?
15. How can you help not to make this divorce become an all-out muckraking battle?
16. What are your fees? Retainer fee? Other charges? How will you bill

CHOOSING AN ATTORNEY

me?

The answers to all of these questions will reveal all that you may want to know about the attorney you are interviewing. Be certain to take careful notes so that you can compare these responses with the responses that other attorneys have made. The answers given by the attorney will tell you how this person runs his/her practice and how effectively s/he relates to clients. Listen carefully to the manner in which the attorney answers the questions as well as the content of these answers. As you listen, you must make decisions as to whether you feel that this person is someone you can trust and someone who will work closely with you. At the end of this consultation you should, based on the answers you have heard, know whether you would feel comfortable considering this attorney as the person that you will want to represent you in court.

Why ask so many comprehensive questions? Divorce law has become a highly specialized field. The cases are not heard in any courtroom by any judge. They are usually heard in the department of Family or Domestic law by judges who have experience in this field of law. The effective and competent cases are also presented by attorneys who have specialized for years. An attorney who does not have the appropriate experience in handling divorce matters will not know the protocols and will undoubtedly foul things up with inexcusable and damaging errors and omissions. If the attorney generally represents men, and you are a woman, it is important to assess whether this person can understand the marital circumstance and problems from your point of view. If an attorney has a background in being an advocate for children, this attorney will certainly have a better understanding of the children's needs with regard to a discussion and agreement concerning custody/visitation.

Therefore, you need to have the expectation that the attorney will keep you continually and completely informed. You will insist on being consulted and having things explained to you thoroughly before any important decisions are to be made. Attorneys like to settle matters and they often make 'deals' and then try to sell them to their clients. You will instruct your attorney that no 'deals' or decisions will ever be made prior to your input. There should be no shyness with regard to asking your attorney questions, giving information or making requests. If you do not choose an attorney who allows you to feel confidence and trust, it will not be possible to talk with the attorney about the intimate facts of the difficulties in the marriage. As an example of one way to choose an attorney (or not to choose an attorney), and the consequences that may be faced, the following vignette is offered:

Jane's husband has moved out and told her that he wants a divorce. Jane did not want the separation or divorce, but she understands clearly and has known for quite some time, that her marriage is over. She decides that she has to accept the situation and get on with her life. She knows that she has to find an attorney so she begins her search. She goes through the yellow pages and picks out a name that sounds good to her because it was her mother's name. She calls and sets up an appointment for the next day. At the time of the appointment Jane began to feel very emotional and unsettled. She was experiencing a difficult and very depressing day. At the consultation with the attorney, Jane cries and it is very apparent that she is emotionally disturbed by the circumstance. The attorney tries to comfort her by telling her that she will take care of the case in its entirety and that Jane should not worry because she would have nothing to do. However, the attorney never asked Jane what she wanted from the divorce or about her attitudes toward her husband and children. Jane, feeling better because she was comforted by this lovely older woman with her mother's name, decided on the spot, no questions asked, to hire this attorney. To her chagrin, after the divorce was well under way, Jane and her attorney had several disagreements as to how to handle certain aspects of the case. Jane is not interested in a fight to the death with her husband. She wants to settle, be treated fairly and treat him fairly. Her attorney turned out to be a zealous advocate who carries feminism to a pathological level and is quite antagonistic toward professional men. Jane's husband is the C.E.O. of a large company and represents many negative concepts to

Jane's attorney. These two aspects of her personality combine, and in her need to get the best of all possible deals for Jane, the attorney begins prolonging the case and making it far more complex than it needs to be.

Jane's story is actually not an atypical one. It could be applied to a male or female lawyer at any time, depending upon the lawyer's personal views. If she had spent the time doing her homework and asking the questions that she needed to ask, she would have discovered the differences in their philosophies. She would have seen that this attorney was not sensitive to her needs but had another agenda that she wanted to impose on Jane's case. This would have led to a more educated decision and she would have realized that the attorney was too zealous and Jane would not have hired this person to represent her in court. If she was too upset to go to the initial appointment, she should have canceled it! In addition, it is to both the client and the attorney's benefit to be certain that all the pertinent philosophical information comes out very early in their relationship. In this manner, the attorney will have more satisfied customers which, of course, will always stimulate more business.

As the divorce gets played out in court, many strong attitudes and feelings come and go. Clients often experience rather serious ups and downs during their divorce. The experienced attorney is prepared for this and able to keep the client focused on the important areas of the divorce.

This means continuous open lines of communication between attorney and client at all times. The client helps by thinking about the divorce and about possible alternative solutions or settlements to resolve the difficulties. The client knows the strengths and weaknesses of the other spouse, and can therefore be highly effective in making suggestions for resolution. This position of cooperation through the sharing of information by both client and attorney permits a better attitude from the beginning. It makes the client far less susceptible to the extremes of emotion experienced by many people in divorces.

Most attorneys will be sympathetic but they usually do not want to fulfill the role of hand-holders or therapists. They generally want to be the legal expert and not the psychological expert. It is difficult for the attorney to handle the emotional aspects of the divorce in addition to all of the legal maneuvers that must take place. In Jane's case, the attorney was clearly not able to deal with her emotional state. It was all right for the attorney to console Jane but the attorney was doing this in order to maintain control of the case rather than out of any emotional connection or support. Jane understood the attorney to be comforting her psychological feelings, calming her and making her feel better. In most cases, attorneys want to spend very little time talking to you about the emotional and psychological aspects of your divorce. Although many clients want to spend time talking to their attorneys about their anxieties and psychological pain, this is rarely a topic that is productive. A psychologically aware and sophisticated attorney will know when to suggest to the client that s/he should seek outside professional mental health counseling. This attorney recognizes that stress must be reduced in a professional and appropriate manner. Clients who become involved with counseling early in their divorce inevitably feel better throughout the process and they will heal faster once it is over.

Jane and her attorney had disagreements and the case was not going the way that Jane would have liked. The attorney was taking the role of deciding what was best for Jane rather than Jane making these decisions for herself. This is why the discussion regarding divorce philosophies in general, and your case in specific, must be held early in the attorney-client relationship. The process of effective and clear communication between client and attorney is critical. The most frequent complaints clients have regarding their spouse is "lack of communication". The most frequent complaint we hear concerning family law attorneys is "lack of communication". Clients are often heard to say things like, "I can't get my attorney on the phone. They do not let me know what is happening in my case. They do not seem to be doing anything".

Divorce is clearly a traumatic experience for both of the divorcing parties. The outcome of the divorce process will undoubtedly have long-range consequences for everyone concerned. Hire the attorney whose ideas and style most correspond with your own and with whom you feel the most comfortable. This process should transcend costs. The divorce is too important to cut financial corners. When one considers the cost of the wedding, the cost of the divorce may not look quite so bad.

If an individual cannot afford to hire an attorney, this person can get valuable information from the initial consultation. Ask the attorney what other services might be available to you if you cannot afford his/her full fee. Some attorneys will advise you on a consulting basis so you do not have to pay a retainer fee and you essentially handle the case yourself. However, you consult with the attorney when you need to. Most courts will have a pro per clinic where you can get good information and guidance to represent yourself. Often an attorney will have the opportunity to supervise an assistant or paralegal that might do a large percentage of the work at reduced costs. The attorney might also know about a legal assistance program that may be administered by the local bar or by a local law school. Frequently attorneys will volunteer to staff a free clinic on a rotating basis so that low or no cost legal information can be offered to the public. The more traditional Legal Aid Program found in the phone book may also be of benefit to you. The larger firms will usually have an attorney on staff who works on a pro bono or unpaid status. See if any of these avenues are open in order to help to solve some of your difficulties.

Many larger cities have specific family law programs which are administered through a charitable organization that will offer either low cost or no cost divorces. This information can also be found in the yellow pages of your local community telephone book. The local Family Law Bar Association should also know about these services.
Prior to establishing your divorce as a knock-down-drag-out, win-lose battle where the children are forced to take a particular side, it is wise to consider mediation or arbitration as a viable alternative. Many states now require mediation services prior to appearing in court. In this manner there might be agreements reached early in the process. If you feel that your spouse is amenable to working out an agreement with a mediator, this opportunity should be utilized without hesitation. The mediator can also guide you to an attorney, legal assistant or

typing service that will properly and inexpensively prepare your legal documents once an agreed-upon stipulation has been reached.
We recommend that after mediation the services of an attorney be utilized on an hourly basis to be absolutely certain that all papers and stipulations are properly filed with the Court. An attorney can be hired for a relatively inexpensive fee to prepare the documents. In this way you will be certain that your rights are being protected and that the documents are being correctly filed. This is especially important if the marital community has a great deal of property to dissolve or if there are minor children whose rights need to be protected as well. Why not spend a small amount of money to be certain that everything is done correctly so that you and your spouse and your children are protected from future legal problems, continued misunderstandings or perhaps even hastily reached agreements that you cannot live with successfully? An attorney will be able to guide you and seal the agreements with professional awareness and correct legal regard for everyone's rights. In this situation, it is extremely important to choose an attorney that is "mediation friendly". Many experienced lawyers are, but there are also many who tell you they can get you a better deal outside of mediation. This usually results in far more attorney fees being paid with little positive result. You can ask your mediator about specific lawyers to determine if they are friendly with the process. The lawyer you want should be able to give you advice, suggest revisions to a proposed agreement that are in your best interests, but still work within the mediation process so that your case is completed through mediation.

   Another relatively new and exciting approach to divorce is the Collaborative Divorce Process. Many local County Bar Associations now provide a list of lawyers trained in this approach. Essentially, it is a merging of mediation and attorney representation. Each spouse hires his/her own lawyer who is a participant in this process. All four, husband, wife and both lawyers, agree that the case will be resolved outside the courtroom and specifically agree not to go to court. In fact, if the wife and husband, or one of them, decides to leave the collaborative process at some point and take their case to court, each person must hire a new lawyer to do so. The purpose of this is to encourage people to handle their divorce cases outside of court and in a more cooperative atmosphere. In the collaborative process, the attorneys and spouses get together for joint meetings and agree in advance to have a complete, open disclosure of all things relating to their divorce. There is no adversarial mentality and the parties are specifically instructed to "play nice" and cooperate with the other. The attorneys encourage this while still being able to competently protect the rights of their respective clients and bring the case to a fair resolution.

Collaborative Law is gaining momentum as a method of choice for divorcing couples because they commit to resolve their case outside of court, cooperate with lawyers who are clearly willing to do so, attempt to end their relationship in a more positive and less hostile way, and spend far less money in doing so. This process is highly recommended in most cases because each person has their own lawyer to protect their interests but stay out of the adversary court battle.

CHAPTER 4
LEGAL PROCEDURES FOR DIVORCE

Divorce is a legal process as well as a psychological experience. It is very necessary, even if you are well represented by counsel, to educate yourself so that you are very familiar with the general legal procedures and laws. There is no uniform code of laws that covers divorce in all states. It is unfortunate that laws and procedures differ from state to state. This often presents a problem when one of the parties has moved or is planning to move to another part of the country. In addition, the issue is sometimes further compounded when both of the parties attempt to file their divorce in different courts in different states. The best way to find out about the divorce laws of your state is to consult with an attorney. If you are a research-minded person and enjoy doing things yourself, you can go to the county courthouse where there is a law library and do some reading and research.

The divorce begins when a specific document is filed with the court. This is called a complaint or a petition. Your attorney will prepare this document from the information you supply. If you are representing yourself, then you will get this document from the county courthouse and prepare it yourself, or you may hire a divorce service or paralegal to complete this project if you have almost no assets to divide nor any children. When the papers are completely prepared, they are taken to the county clerk. A modest fee which is determined locally accompanies these papers and they are filed. The fee you have paid covers the privilege of having a specific file opened in your name which holds what is now called your 'moving papers'. This is the official beginning of your divorce and the first step of many specific steps which are to follow. The document must now be served on your spouse either directly or by serving it on your spouse's attorney. The serving of the complaint is also handled in a very specific and prescribed manner. Some person who is not connected with the case in any manner, and who is over the age of eighteen years old, must be employed to handle this project. This person must physically hand over the court papers to your spouse or to his/her agent who will be the attorney. There are many private process serving agencies which can be hired to accomplish this task. Although their charges may vary, one can usually expect to spend about $50.00 for this service. The Sheriff or Marshall's department in your local county will also accomplish this task for a nominal fee of approximately $20.00. When your spouse has been officially served, you will receive a notice that the task has been accomplished. Once this is done, an answer will be forthcoming from your spouse sometime within a period of thirty days.

    Your spouse will file a response which constitutes an answer to your moving papers. A copy of this response will then be delivered directly to you if you are representing yourself, or directly to the office of your attorney. Sometimes, if you and your spouse are friendly, having an amicable divorce, and expect to establish a working agreement, responsive papers need not be filed during this time period. If papers are not filed, be certain to get a written agreement on this from your spouse if you are the party who was served the original papers. If you make the unfortunate error of assuming that this agreement exists, and it is not written, it can have disastrous implications. When the time requirement comes and goes without a response being filed by you, then your spouse who originally filed can take your default. This means that your spouse can go into court and ask for whatever s/he wishes because no response was filed. Therefore, if you are the person served with the divorce papers, be certain to meet the time requirements and be certain that you do this whether or not you have had the time to hire an attorney.

The State of California as well as some other states has a procedure which is called a summary dissolution. This is a quick and easy procedure which may be utilized by the parties. If both parties agree on how to divide the property, and if there are no children or houses or large debts, they may be able to utilize the summary dissolution procedure. This procedure costs very little and does not require the services of attorneys. It is simple, uncomplicated, and a very specific procedure established just for couples with little or no community property. Many young couples who, after a short marriage, have decided that the marriage was a mistake, and who have not yet accumulated a great deal of property, may utilize this procedure.

There are two other very definite processes which may be used to dissolve marital relationships. These are: a nullity of marriage (called an annulment); and a legal separation. The specific names of these procedures may vary from state to state. Some states may also have other procedures which are peculiar to the region rather than more universal as these are. An annulment is filed if you have the desire to declare that your marriage is void, or that it never existed at all. If the judge grants your request to annul your marriage, then it is as if your marriage never took place and never existed. Each state has specific requirements that must be met prior to the granting of an annulment. These requirements may include: a short marriage which was decided on after a very brief period of time of the parties knowing each other; no children between the parties; or perhaps one of the parties had misrepresented something which may be very important to the other party. This might include one of the parties not telling the other that s/he was already married in another state, or that a previous divorce was never completed. Under these conditions, an annulment is appropriate.

The reason is that one is always precluded by law from marrying if one is already actually married. Marrying two people at the same time is bigamy and highly illegal in every state. In addition, an annulment will usually be granted by the court if one can demonstrate the parties married as a joke, or if one of the parties utilized some coercion or if there was extreme stress involved in the initial reasons for the marriage.

A legal separation accomplishes almost everything a divorce does. In a legal separation, the judge has the capacity to: divide the community or marital property for the separating couple; approve an agreed-upon property settlement made by the parties; award spousal and child support payments; and make custody and visitation orders. These are all the normal procedures which take place when a divorce is granted. The only thing that a legal separation does not accomplish is that it does not terminate the marriage. A legal separation may be very appropriate in situations of religious conflicts where the parties are opposed to divorce but wish to separate from each other in their property and no longer wish to live together. There are times when financial reasons may motivate people to utilize the route of legal separation rather than divorce. The experience of most attorneys is that when a legal separation occurs, it will, in the near future, usually be converted to a complete divorce action. Certainly this will happen if one of the parties wishes to marry someone else. Recall that a new marriage cannot take place legally until a divorce occurs, thereby completely breaking the old marriage bond.

The type of legal separation we are discussing should be carefully distinguished from an actual, physical separation. There are some very specific legal consequences that can take place when a couple actually separates from one another, whether or not they have filed any formal legal papers. For example, when a couple actually separates, the money each party earns or the debts that each party incurs, usually becomes their own individual responsibility and not their spouse's responsibility. There are times when couples may agree that they want to live separately but they feel that they must remain in the same home because they do not have the funds for one member of the couple to move out and become completely independent. In these cases, they will set up housekeeping in different rooms, no longer share a bed, and they agree that they are no longer considering themselves to be a married couple. They view each other as separate, single people. There are other couples who may decide that they wish to work on dealing with the issues of their marriage but they feel that this can only be done if they live apart. In this case they may not consider themselves to be completely and officially separated. It is apparent that the attitude of the parties is most important and that it sets the stage for the type of separation they will have.

Although some people may wish to elaborate their reasons for getting a divorce, most states now neither require nor do they actually permit you to make these reasons public. These states subscribe to a set of laws which are called "no fault divorce laws". Within this philosophy, neither member of the divorcing couple is considered to be at fault for the dissolution of the marriage. In most cases each of the parties believes that the other is at fault. Even when this does occur, the judge does not wish to hear about it because it does not matter with regard to the divorce decisions that the judge must make. Checking with your attorney can educate you as to the specific laws of your own state with regard to no-fault divorce.

Either member of the couple can request a judge to grant temporary orders whether they have filed for a divorce, an annulment or a legal separation. A temporary order is an order from the court which will make certain orders and establish certain groundrules for the parties to follow that will be in effect prior to and until the next court hearing, or the final judgment. These can be orders regarding temporary custody of the children and visitation of the children; child and spousal support payments; restricting one spouse from coming near another spouse (temporary restraining order); or stopping one or both of the parties from selling or otherwise disposing of any of the property that they may have in common.

As an example of the above, we recently saw a couple who were divorcing over many negative issues. One of these was the fact that the husband has a very elaborate workshop with the most professional of tools in his garage where he spends a great deal of his time. Most of his tools were purchased after the marriage and, therefore, are part of the community assets. When he left the home, he took very little. He was fearful that his wife would sell his tools in a spiteful move to upset him. He requested a court order which was granted forbidding his wife from selling, giving away, or otherwise disposing of any of his prized tools. Since no agreements have been reached by the parties early in the dissolution these orders have been requested from the court. With this available, neither of the spouses can violate the court order and so neither can do anything to the other which would be considered to be unfair or harmful within these parameters. Orders of the judge can be requested by either spouse at any hearing after filing the initial complaint or petition. For example:

Sara had her attorney request that the judge order her husband, John, to keep away from her home and also not disturb her at her work place. She did this because she is fearful that his anger may lead to him trying to harm her. The judge grants this request before a hearing in court but also sets a specific hearing date to deal with other issues as well as this particular one. At that time both Sara and John must appear in court to tell the judge why they feel that the existing orders should or should not be kept in place. When Sara's attorney first makes this request, he does not do it in a formal, open court hearing. Instead, he goes to the judge's chambers and talks to the judge privately. Any orders that are obtained in this manner must be served on the other party so that both parties know what has transpired.

Either spouse also has the right to request that a hearing date be set so that s/he can then request certain orders from the judge. These orders can include those previously discussed or perhaps other areas such as how the parties can be cooperative in order to get certain community bills paid. At this hearing, the judge will listen to the attorneys' arguments and then decide whether or not to grant the requests. These orders differ from the previous orders since they were initially obtained prior to the more formal hearing. Orders obtained before a formal hearing are termed "emergency orders" and will stay in place until the formal hearing. These types of requests for orders are more unusual and request immediate action by the Judge. New orders can be granted at the time of the formal hearing. The method utilized to get the judge to make certain orders depends very much on the sense of urgency the party feels and how necessary they believe it is to obtain this order. Any orders obtained while the divorce is ongoing must be considered seriously by the parties as very specific rules by which they now have to adjust to and live their lives. It is important to be aware of the fact that if you are served with papers that are requesting orders from the court, you must file your responsive papers within a very short period of time.

CHILD CUSTODY

Early in the couples' separation it is important for the judge to make child custody and visitation orders. The judge has the power to determine where the children of a marriage will live and how often and for how long a period of time they will see each parent. This does not mean that the children will have the right to decide where they shall live. The judge makes the decision only after hearing the information provided by both parents and sometimes, in more adversarial cases, attorneys appointed to represent the children. More and more we have been seeing judges who are appointing an attorney to represent the children so that they can directly present evidence on their behalf. Even with all of these people trying to use their most persuasive arguments, a judge may also not be able to come to resolution with regard to the custody/visitation issue. At this time an expert psychologist may be appointed, stipulated to by both parties, and a psychological custody evaluation will then take place. In some states, like California for example, it is mandatory for the parents and children to meet with a court mediator to try to work out a custodial plan before going into court. If they can, then that plan is adopted by the Judge. If they cannot, then the Judge will make the determination as to a custodial plan.

In cases where more than one state is involved, there are state and federal laws that will govern which state will have the jurisdiction and therefore be able to hear the custody/visitation orders. There are also very specific state and federal laws which prohibit one from kidnapping one's own child and removing the child from the area in order to prevent the other parent from having contact. Parents are usually encouraged by the court system to come to an agreement with regard to custody and visitation of their children as quickly as possible. If the parents are foolish enough to sabotage each other or if they cannot come to an agreement by themselves or with a mediator, a private psychologist may be appointed to do a complete evaluation of the family. When the psychologist finishes interviewing and testing all the members of the family, s/he sends a report to the judge with copies to both attorneys and to the court mediator. The information collected by the psychologist and the recommendations that are made are then used by the judge to help resolve the custody/visitation dispute. Oftentimes both attorneys will recognize that agreements can not be reached between the parties, and they will work together and recommend that a psychologist be stipulated to and hired by the parents, to complete an impartial evaluation. This is in preparation for the court hearing and will then be used to allow the judge some specific recommendations from a neutral professional party as to what is in the best interests of the children. This choice requires that the parties have a full blown court hearing which is costly and always requires a great deal of preparation before hand. This may mean trying to dig up examples of why and how your spouse is a bad parent or a bad person, and therefore should spend limited time with the children. It will undoubtedly mean that the attorneys will urge the parties to hire expert professional psychologists and psychiatrists to tell the judge why s/he believes that one or the other is the best parent. It also means taking depositions, bringing in character witnesses in person or in the form of declarations, thereby airing all of the family difficulties in a public hearing. At rare times the children are also brought into the courtroom to testify. This is an extremely traumatic circumstance for them and should be avoided at all costs. Responsible attorneys will counsel their clients that the emotional and financial traumas which arise from these experiences are often lifelong. We agree absolutely that forcing children into court to testify either for or against a parent in open court is a serious mistake and a circumstance to be avoided. Remember, it is always better to reach an agreement through discussion, negotiation and mediation than through a knockdown and drag-out court hearing. This is especially true when the issues revolve around the future of your children. You are cautioned to put other things aside and take care of your own children rather than to allow a judge to make those life decisions. Unfortunately, the State of California is in the process of passing and formalizing legislation that will allow children of certain ages to testify in the courtroom. This legislation has been passed by very short-sighted people who are obviously not familiar with the divorce process and the impact of forcing children to take sides by testifying in court. Very few experienced, competent family law attorneys support this disturbing approach.

There are situations where a parent has been emotionally or physically abusive to a child. If this occurs, it requires a judge to intervene. If one parent has been abusive to the children and refuses to admit it or seek help, or if one parent is psychologically unfit to parent, then this will have to be resolved through a court hearing. In such a matter, one parent will wish to demonstrate to the judge why the other parent should not have custody or should be limited or supervised in visitation with the child.

It has been our experience that if the parents are able to put aside their own angers and their own needs for revenge, they can focus on the needs of their child. When this happens they are usually able to come up with an agreement which is satisfactory to all concerned. Any agreement arrived at can be altered at a later date if the situation changes and demands a new agreement. This allows the parents a good measure of flexibility as the child grows and their needs change. Any change can be agreed upon and then filed with the court and made an order which is then incorporated into the court file. When a judge makes an order that order cannot be modified without a hearing in front of that judge and a new order. Therefore, it is easy to see that the best agreements are reached privately between the parents. Using the mediator or a private professional as a facilitator is usually an excellent idea.

Parents must remember that children always suffer in all divorces. No matter how healthy the children and no matter how smoothly the parents can work in court, the children will not come away unscathed. Children never want their parents to be separated and they will attempt many subtle tricks to get them back together. Most divorcing parents do not fight over the children but they frequently will use the children and the custody issue as a power play to get back at the other spouse. If divorcing parents were to actually spend time thinking about this before making the decision to fight over custody and visitation, they would save themselves a great deal of money and they would save their children a great deal of anxiety. They do not seem to realize or care that this type of experience can easily result in the children experiencing long-term, serious emotional disturbance.

Some examples of child custody terms are as follows:

Legal Custody. This describes the ability of the parent or parents together to make decisions regarding their children in areas such as: where they will live; which doctors they will see; where they will attend school; where they will attend church; and many other decisions regarding their general welfare. In a more normal family situation, both parents will have equal input into these decisions. When parents share legal custody, they are expected to make joint and cooperative decisions regarding health services, education and the general welfare of the children. Therefore, these important decisions for the children are made jointly after consultation between both parents. It is only in situations where the parents cannot get along at all nor can they work together to make decisions for the benefit of the children that a Judge will appoint only one of them as the one to make all decisions as outlined above. This also takes place in a situation where one parent has been abusive, molested the children, or the cause of domestic violence.

Physical Custody. This describes who has physical custody of the children or where they actually live. Currently, we speak about a custodial plan for the children, that is, how much time they spend with each parent. The courts are getting away from using the term of "visitation" as that term offends parents who have less time with their children and who do not want to be viewed as "visiting" their children. In a situation where both parents are involved and capable, then they will share a custody arrangement based on their work schedules, where they live, the children's schedules so that they each have a significant amount of time with their children. It does not mean that a "shared or joint" physical custody arrangement is equal as to time, it just means that they each have significant time with their children based on the factors just mentioned. Although the parents divorce each other, this arrangement helps them not to be forced to divorce their children. A joint arrangement keeps both parents active and involved. Many parents are unable to maintain this arrangement due to petty anger and jealousy. Each divorcing family must decide the best plan for their family. Even though the parties are divorced and possibly re-married, we have seen many, many wonderful cooperative joint custodial plans that have most definitely been in the best interests of the children.

If the parents go to a court hearing to allow a judge to decide custody, the judge has a finite number of arrangements from which to choose. If the two parents can come to an agreement, the judge must still approve it in order to see that the children are being protected and that the parents are being fair to the children and to each other. Often, there is more than one child. The literature strongly suggests that siblings should not be split up. However, there are circumstances when it may be appropriate to have different custody/visitation plans for different children. For example, visitation or custody for a newborn infant, a handicapped child, or one with special medical or psychological needs may of necessity be different than the other children. In some cases, it may be better for the child to spend more time with one parent than the other. Children may be bonded differently with each parent. This should be recognized, carefully studied, and taken into consideration when working out the custody/visitation arrangements. As indicated, it is rare to separate siblings. However, if there are large disparities in age, identification and needs, it may be more appropriate to design specific individualized plans for each child. This can be done by the parents themselves or with the assistance of the psychological evaluator. The evaluation attempts to determine the specific needs of each child and then further determines which parent can best meet those needs. It is certainly possible that different parents may be needed for different children. When there is a split of the siblings it is also imperative to design a program where they will have time together so long as there is no psychological or physical danger to any of the siblings present in such a program.

The divorcing couple needs to understand that, under normal conditions, both parents have an absolute right to visit with their children. In addition, the children have an absolute right to have ample time exposure to both parents. There are situations in which visitation may be inappropriate but these are rare. It may occur if one parent has sexually abused or molested a child. It is also possible that one parent has maliciously blocked the other parent's rights to visitation. In these cases the judge may limit visitation to the non-cooperative parent. Most states indicate that the custodial time is not gender based anymore. Instead, it is based on which parent can demonstrate cooperation in permitting ample visitation with the opposite parent. The judge can also assign a supervisor and demand that the parent have rigidly supervised visitation in order to protect the child. The judge has the power to do whatever may be necessary and correct to protect the best interests of the child. The judge's responsibility in a custody matter is to be concerned only with the best interests of the children first and foremost.

In the same way a good and healthy parent cannot be kept away from spending time with his/her child, a disinterested parent cannot be forced to visit with a child. Some divorced parents, for reasons of their own, choose not to see their children. However, when a parent goes to court to get an order to see children, that parent is expected to follow through with the court orders. If a child does not wish to visit a parent, the parent may involve psychological services to help the relationship between parent and child. In addition, as the child gets older and becomes involved in numerous pursuits, friends and school in the primary custodial home, there are practical problems that the non-custodial parent must understand. The non-custodial parent feels rejected but must understand that even if the parents were still together, the child would still be involved in outside pursuits. When a child is consistently refusing to see a parent without any other activities impinging, then there may be some underlying psychological reasons which should be carefully investigated.

As the divorce proceeds and plays itself out, each party begins to move on to a new phase of life. Re-marriage can make major changes in life. It becomes a distinct possibility that this may involve a geographical move, job change or job transfer. When these new circumstances arise, the custodial plan must be re-visited and often changed to accommodate the new situation. The parents should be talking to each other so that they can examine new possibilities. A mediator or therapist trained in issues of custody can be brought in to offer some fresh possibilities that perhaps the parents had not considered. They need to do a great deal of talking to each other so that the children can also be fully prepared appropriately by their parents. A parent who attempts to move with the specific purpose of preventing the other parent from seeing the child runs the risk of forfeiting custody. The courts always encourage both parents to have regular, ongoing contact with their children. When this is blocked, it is equivalent to contempt of the court orders.

A Special Master is a specifically trained Psychologist, Attorney, or other licensed counselor such as a Social Worker. It has been noted that in especially acrimonious divorces, the parties will appear in court almost weekly. Each time there is a disagreement about clothes, sports activities, visitation time, or almost anything, the parties haul each other into court. These matters are easily solved but they clog the calendar and waste a great deal of time. In addition, the parties will often change attorneys and some attorneys will make enormous cases out of a one hour differential in visitation. Some attorneys will schedule depositions, bring in witnesses and go on and on because this is what their client wants. Judges do not wish to see these people. The judge rules that the parties cannot come to court without first consulting the Special Master, but this is usually with the agreement of the parties. The Special Master is not a therapist, not a mediator, not a deal-maker. Instead, the Special Master is an arbitrator trained in professional mental health. S/he does exactly what the judge does, that is to listen to both sides carefully and decide where there is merit with regard to the best interests of the children. Often the Special master will interview the children as well. The Special Master has an advantage since s/he can also contact teachers, therapists, other family members or anyone associated with the particular issues. The Special Master then produces a report outlining the issues and offering very specific recommendations. This report is sent to the judge, the parties and their attorneys. The judge then signs the recommendations as orders of the court unless either party objects. Most parents do not go back to court but instead, they try the Special Master's plan. The Special Master has the advantage of altering the plan to fit the circumstance. This process alleviates a great deal of court congestion and gives the parents much more direct access to a person who can institute change immediately. Our Special Master clients come fairly frequently at first but the issues mellow rapidly when they see how quickly things can be resolved. Without the attorneys and a formal court setting, the process becomes smoother and easier. The author has Special Master clients that they have not seen for years at a time.

DIVISION OF THE COMMUNITY ASSETS

The division of the community or marital property owned in the marriage is an important concern of every divorcing couple. Since the specific laws dealing with property division vary from state to state, some research has to be accomplished by the divorcing couple. If you have both hired attorneys, they will extend their counsel to you regarding the rights of each party. If there are no attorneys it would be wise to go to the law library to review the literature regarding the laws of your particular state. In most states, property which is acquired by the married couple together during the time of the marriage is considered to be marital or community property. This property may take many forms such as gifts received or things purchased with the money earned during the marriage. Property received by one spouse, or items inherited by one spouse, may be considered to be the separate property of that spouse and will ordinarily not be divided up by the court during the court proceedings. However, all property which is considered as marital property will be divided up by the court. With this in mind, it is apparent that it makes far more sense for the divorcing couple to come to some fair agreement on the division of their property. If they can not agree, the judge will do it for them. If you allow the judge to divide your property, you lose complete control over what you and your spouse receive. Some items will have to be sold if the judge acts and these items may be the very things that you might wish to keep. The author encourages couples to call a truce and set aside their animosity for each other so that they can work out their own property division agreements. Although one might think this impossible, it can work and we have seen the angriest of all couples put things aside to make certain that they each protected their own interests. At times a professional mediator can be of great assistance in this matter. One suggestion with regard to dividing the property is to inventory the items together. At the same time, a fair market value should be agreed upon and placed on each item. Once this has been accomplished, the couple can meet and each chooses an item, agreeing to alternate their choices until the job has been completed. Since you have placed a fair market value on each item, you can arrange it so that you will each end up with about the same dollar value of the property. Do not assume that it means either the purchase price or the replacement values of the items.

    The fair market value approach must also be used with regard to current debts on specific items of property. For example, let us assume that Ned and Jane bought a new refrigerator two years ago for $550.00. Now they are getting a divorce and they are ready to divide up their property. The refrigerator is worth $325.00 at this time, however, they still owe $200.00. The net fair market value then becomes $125.00.

Many times there will be insufficient funds or property to make a relatively equal division of the marital property without selling the family home. Most people have their major financial asset tied up in the equity in their home. Selling the home where you have lived for a considerable period of time may be an extremely difficult psychological process. However, if it becomes the only choice so that the property can be divided, then it must be done. As we have stated, it is better to come to an agreement with your spouse than to have the divorce court divide up your property.

It is also possible to continue to own a home jointly if it will be more financially beneficial. It might be utilized as a rental which would then throw off some income as well as long term capital gains. The watchword with regard to the division of community property is to be creative and come up with solutions with which you can both live and which the judge might not even have thought of or considered. Sometimes, one spouse will have owned the home prior to the marriage. It is also possible that the couple was not married when the home was purchased and while cohabiting, or that one spouse may have put down a lot more money than the other at the time of the purchase. In these situations, with a short marriage, you each may have a different percentage interest in the home. This becomes reflected after the sale when each member of the couple will receive different amounts of money depending on their particular percent of their ownership.

In addition to the family home, another major asset of the marriage is often the retirement plan or pension plan one or both of the parties might have through their place of employment. Although it might not come into play for many years, it is still a value that must be considered. In fact it must be considered at the time of the divorce since a specific amount must be agreed upon. These plans grow significantly over the years and the values after the divorce belong to only the party with the plan. This can be divided equally or used as a trade-off against other property or assets such as the value of the family home.

DEALING WITH THE MARITAL DEBT

Debts of the marriage are usually treated in the same manner as the positive values of the marital property. If there is a debt on a particular item of property such as a car or a condominium, then the person receiving the property will usually also receive the debt. Debts can be used to equalize the division of property. In other words, if one of you is going to receive a larger value of your marital property, it would also be fair for that person to receive a larger share of the marital debts. Otherwise, debts can be divided up equally. This may include credit card bills, medical expenses, or loans. Any method of assigning debt can be used which the couple thinks is fair. If one of you has a greater earning capacity than the other, more debts may be assigned to this spouse. The same rule applies to the marital property. Although a judge may divide up the debts and property utilizing a computer program, it is still far better to accomplish this yourselves and be able to offer an already agreed upon stipulation to the judge which then will automatically become the orders of the court.

SPOUSAL SUPPORT

When one spouse pays money to the other, it is usually characterized as either alimony or spousal support. This means that the money is paid directly to the receiving spouse or to a specifically designated third party. Money paid to a third party can be directed toward a variety of needs such as rent, mortgage payments, medical needs, auto or other payments. The purpose of spousal support payments is to permit the spouse receiving the money to maintain a particular lifestyle as similar as possible to that which was enjoyed during the marriage. However, it is important to remember that in a typical divorce there will be less money to go around after the separation. Although both of the parties are entitled to maintain their lifestyles, this is usually not practical or reality based. It will usually be more difficult to do so because of the drain on the finances. This will have to be accepted and both parties have to make appropriate adjustments so that the previous single household assets can now support two households.

The amount of the spousal support payments is usually dependent on the length of the marriage in concert with the needs of the receiving spouse and the ability of the paying spouse. The longer the marriage, the longer the spousal support term. A large difference in incomes between the partners may also mean a larger payment. The earning capacity of each of the parties is also an important consideration. Areas to consider may be the job training skills of the parties, education, job availability, and needs. All of these areas and more must be taken into consideration by the divorce court when the judge fixes the amount of spousal support to be paid. Many states have formulae that judges use to help them set the amount of support. It is interesting that this area tends to be somewhat inconsistent and will vary from state to state and even from judge to judge in the same area. Although there are computer formulae and tables which are regularly utilized, the amounts can differ depending on the agreed upon amounts which are plugged into the formula. Be prepared for this lack of consistency.

Ronald is a bank manager and Jane is a homemaker who has been caring for their two children in a traditional marriage. The children are both in elementary school and Jane is now free to work. Ronald, upset about the breakup of their marriage, wants to live in another city where he will have to take a job as a bank teller because there are no managerial or supervisorial positions available. Taking this job will mean that he will receive only half of his current pay. Jane was a schoolteacher before the marriage and she has a valid grade credential so that she is well able to get a job teaching. Since Ronald is the party who wants to relocate, he may very well have to pay spousal support based on his income as a manager. If he chooses to relocate and work for less money, this is his choice and Jane should not suffer from this. However, Jane may be required to return to teaching so that she can bring in money for her own support as well. The major point in this example is that both Ronald and Jane will have to do the best they can to produce income. If Ronald were to be transferred by his company and have no choice in the matter, he might be able to pay Jane less for a lesser paying job. Since he chooses to lower his own standard of living, he does not necessarily have the right to significantly and arbitrarily lower Jane's living standards. Handling the spousal support payments in this manner will discourage the upset husband or wife from punishing the opposite spouse by purposely changing jobs to earn less money. It also encourages the other spouse to earn money by assessing a figure based on ability to earn.

Spousal support ends when the spouse receiving the money remarries. Additionally, the parties or the court can set a specific date when support will end. The support amounts can be changed if there is an appropriate and realistic change in the financial condition of the parties. For example, if the paying spouse is laid off from work or receives a raise, the amount can change. It will also change significantly if the paying spouse wins the state lottery. Support can be changed by a written agreement between the parties or by going back to court and having the judge utilize the computerized approach to make the decision as to the new amount.

CHILD SUPPORT

Child support is a very specific phrase. It is the payment of money by one spouse to another spouse or to a designated third party specifically for the benefit of the child. Support payments to third parties could be for numerous items such as day care, private schooling or medical payments.

Parents have a legal obligation to support their children until they reach their majority which, in most states, is either age eighteen or twenty-one. This is dependent on the individual's state of residence. In addition, there are many states that require that the parent support the child until the completion of high school regardless of the child's age. Handicapped or disabled children may be supported for longer periods of time depending on the limitations of the child and the court's assessment of the child's ability to be independent in the future. Adult children who become handicapped may also file for child support from their parents if the parents have assets making them capable. Child support can also end if the child becomes an emancipated minor, or decides to be self-supporting and refuses the support. When one refers to his/her children, this includes all biological children, legally adopted children, legitimate or illegitimate children and also children conceived but not yet born.

Most states have a formula utilized by judges and lawyers as a guide which determines how much child support should be paid. The major factors taken into consideration in these formulas are: the earnings of each spouse; the number of children to be supported; and the amount of time the child spends with each parent.

Sue and Tim have three children, a thirteen-year-old boy, and two younger girls, ages eleven and four. Sue has been employed as an accountant and Tim is employed as a schoolteacher. Sue earns about thirty percent more money than Tim. Sue and Tim are amicably trying to work out the conditions of their divorce. After long discussions and consultation with the children, the couple decides that their son will live primarily with Tim while the girls will be spending more of their time with their mother. Visitation schedules are worked out so that each parent will be spending significant time with all of the children. This makes it difficult to figure out the child support payments. Any formula will have to take into consideration the actual custody/visitation arrangement agreed upon as well as the income levels of the parents, their debts and their existing assets and property. Parents can be highly creative with regard to solving the problem of child support because as noted by this very common example, the issue can be highly complicated.

Payments of spousal support and child support can overlap. In some states there is an additional category called family support. With this category, there are no specific dollar amounts allocated to either spousal or child support but rather just one payment covering all of the responsibilities. The issues of support and specific divorce procedures depend greatly on the state in which the divorce takes place. In addition there is always the question of how to handle taxes. An ex-spouse receiving spousal support must claim this as ordinary income. The payer of course, is able to deduct these amounts. However, payments designated as child support are not deductible. In some states the family support payments now cover the tax issues. When payments are made under the 'family support' label, the court will usually make the judgment as to how much may be taxable and reportable income. Keeping in mind the tax issues, the yearly tax deductions for the minor children are negotiable between the parties. When deciding how to allot support, couples need to take all of these aspects into consideration. The parties can work out equitable and creative contracts and the judge will approve these agreements. Coming to a personal, family-oriented agreement including the aspects of custody/visitation, spousal and child support, and property division will make the divorce far easier. Consulting a mediator to assist in this process will certainly be of value. Once an agreement has been worked out, it is wise to take it to your attorney for review prior to signing. In this way, the attorney can help to show you how to protect your rights and can also help to make the agreement palatable to the judge.

Judges tend to enjoy couples who have worked out equitable agreements which have their attorney's blessings. In this way the judge can satisfy everyone by accepting the agreement. The judge does not have to get involved in the formulae which may turn out not to be equitable depending upon the needs of the family and the specific needs of the children. It is always best to bring to the judge a ready-made agreement that everyone can live with than it is to depend on the judge to work out a decision for you. If it is left up to the court you may feel that the decision is not truly equitable and someone or everyone will be unhappy, jealous and resentful. These are common phenomenon and can be avoided if the couple will work diligently at making good business decisions concerning their equity and the payments that must take place in order to adequately support their children.

CHAPTER 5
MEDIATING YOUR DIVORCE

The process of mediation has become an excellent option and it is being utilized with more frequency by couples who are facing divorce. Mediation becomes an even more attractive proposition when we take into consideration the many problems that are faced. These problems include: the very high financial and emotional costs inherent in lawsuits; the long wait to get the case to court; the many steps that have to be completed; the paperwork; and the adversarial nature of the divorce court. Looking at these aspects, it is clear to see why mediation becomes a wonderful alternative. In addition, mediation appointments can be set at a time certain while the courthouse often becomes a frustration-laden place where cases are trailed for hours or days before they can get to a hearing. Mediation is unique in that it can also allow the children some input into the process which usually does not occur if it goes to a court hearing. In most family court sessions, the children are virtually ignored, treated as objects or property, or used by angry parents as pawns in the game of manipulating each other. A good mediator can give the divorcing parents objective insights so that they can see the issues from their children's point of view. This can make it far easier to resolve the very difficult issues of custody and visitation.

A private mediation process is always a voluntary procedure. The divorcing couple recognizes the value of coming together with a neutral third party to attempt to completely resolve their conflicts and thereby avoid the courtroom entirely. It is interesting to note that a successful mediation depends more on the mediator than on the specific divorcing couple. The parties do not have to like each other or even care about each other at all. The only thing that they need to do is to have a strong desire to work out a settlement and a desire to keep out of court and away from the money draining, time consuming, and emotionally antagonistic situation. Mediators will usually charge on an hourly basis for the sessions as well as the preparation of a settlement document. Although the fees will vary just as attorneys' or psychologists' fees vary throughout the country, it will most definitely be less costly in the long run than it would be for a full-blown litigation. A mediator can assist you and your spouse to find creative and satisfying solutions to the difficulties and to the misunderstandings in perception which always occur during the divorce process. Mediators are usually attorneys or psychologists who have had specific training in conflict resolution techniques. Just as in selecting any other profession, remember to get referrals, discuss the credentials, training, and experience of the mediator before agreeing to hire this person.

Mediation will almost always work as long as the parties are able to demonstrate some level of positive motivation. It works specifically because it allows both members of the divorcing couple to be in control of their own destiny. It permits continuous input and the open exchange of information. Problems can be articulated and worked out without being concerned about sanctions from the other side and without being concerned about 'tipping your hand'. A settlement can be worked out or the couple can simply stop the process and back away at any time they wish. The mediator takes on the role of translator, communicator and facilitator. The mediator will make certain that the items you desire to be communicated to your spouse will, in fact, be communicated. This is an excellent way to deal with the intimidation many individuals feel as a hangover from the marriage. The mediator will work to keep the anger down, the intimidation away, and promote clear and creative thinking. This process will give you the opportunity to direct your own input which is unlike the court system.

The first party of the couple who hires an attorney immediately becomes involved in the legal system. This individual will be responsible for legal and court costs and, either unwillingly or willingly, that person will become embroiled in the adversarial mode. Far too frequently, divorce clients lose control over their own cases. Many are forced to watch by the sidelines as the lawyers and judges decide how their lives and their children's lives will be lived. Many times one of the spouses will attempt to talk to the other only to find that an attorney has instructed that spouse that s/he is not to talk. This obviously hampers effective communication and makes meaningful settlement discussions between the parties quite impossible. This situation can be avoided by utilizing the mediation process because it is specifically designed not to be adversarial in nature. The object of the legal system is to bring resolution and order through the proven age-old method of appealing to authority. However, often we see the result manifested in keeping the parties separated, non-communicative and out of control. The object of the mediation process is always to get the parties together, to create and enhance effective communication, and for the couple to be able to devise a cooperative and workable agreement together.

Mediation takes place in a private mediator's office which is viewed as neutral territory, a private and safe place. Attorneys should not be present during the discussions. The parties must agree prior to the beginning that all the material discussed will be held in confidence. In this way, if the mediation process should break down, and the case does eventually go to court, the mediator will not be called as a witness and will not be able to testify unless both parties agree and request the mediator's presence in writing. Feelings, as well as content issues that are not usually discussed in the attorney's office or in the courtroom, can be brought up in mediation. Because the mediator is a trained person in dealing with all aspects of intense emotionality, these feelings can be eliminated from the discussion so that they do not interfere with coming to a fair settlement. Mediation is not psychotherapy and the purpose is not to utilize behavioral or dynamic interpretations to heighten emotional and psychological health. However, the thorough discussion of these emotions does serve to salve the rough edges and remove the major impediments to reaching an agreement. Most couples in the throes of a divorce have a great deal of anger, hostility, bitterness, frustration and disappointment. By allowing these feelings to come out and helping the parties see from where they arise, the mediator can remove significant blocks to working out an agreement. Both overt and covert anger can frequently control and even directly sabotage settlement discussions. However, when some of it goes away, this may be all that is necessary for clearer heads to prevail and agreements to be reached.

There are many different styles within a successful mediation process. Mediators use scientific conflict resolution techniques. However, different mediators will have their favorite ways of dealing with conflict and of resolving disputes. The parties must feel comfortable with the mediator and feel trust in this person. A competent, professional mediator will deal not only with the words being said by the couple, but also will deal with the underlying messages which is where the major stumbling blocks to settlement usually lie. The mediator will encourage the parties to express the important areas of both content and feelings and will help them to communicate these areas to each other. Divorce is always a very highly emotionally charged experience. Because of these qualities, it is very difficult for the divorcing couple to find solutions. Their problems appear to them as being insurmountable. The mediator deals with agreements and sees nothing as insurmountable. The mediator will explore and discuss common ground and suggest new and different creative alternatives that the divorcing couple had not previously considered. The amount of time needed to reach agreements is usually based on motivation, willingness of the parties to set aside their angers and frustrations, and the level of cooperation. Regardless of the amount of time it takes to reach a settlement agreement through mediation, the couple will still have spent less time, money and emotionality than if they had chosen litigation and the adversarial system.

The mediation process should end with a signed agreement which benefits the children. In a good agreement, neither parent will be completely satisfied because it will require that both will have to make some sacrifices. The mediator will point this out, help to smooth ruffled feathers and help the parents to keep the focus on the best interests of the children and not on their own needs. After you have reached an agreement and before you sign anything, it is very wise to seek out the services of a competent attorney. The attorney's job will be to review the agreement with you and then to prepare the legal documents which are necessary to finalize the divorce. Some mediation services will offer to accomplish this for you. However, the author agrees that the best practice is for both parties to have individual attorneys who will look over the agreement. In this manner it will serve to protect both parties, make certain that no rights are being violated and that the mediation agreement is fair to all concerned. If you do not have an attorney already on standby, the mediator can probably give you a referral to an attorney who favors the mediation process and who will understand your needs at this point. Do not be swayed by the attorney who talks about getting a better deal by going to court. If this happens, consult again with your mediator. Often, the only person who gets a better deal when you go to court is the attorney. This attorney may not be interested primarily in your welfare or in your child's needs. If in fact, the agreement reached is not an equal agreement, this needs to be seriously discussed with the attorney. This may occur but there also may be a very good reason for this that only the divorcing parties know about. However, it is the attorney's duty to protect your rights by carefully pointing these things out to you. After appropriate discussion and deliberation of the positives and negatives, you can make an informed decision as to whether this agreement will really accomplish the agreed upon goals. Signing an agreement that is not exactly equal is perfectly appropriate because the world is never equal or exactly fair. There may be specific reasons why you would go along with an unequal agreement. You may be the emotionally healthier person, or you may have greater earning capacity, or you may be physically healthier. There are many important considerations which enter into the agreement process. If you have chosen your attorney prior to the mediation, be certain that you have chosen an attorney who can see and understand that there are other methods available to an individual to resolve conflicts besides the traditional court litigation process.

Choosing a mediator may be easier than choosing an attorney because there are fewer mediators and they are less well known. Mediation as a full time profession is relatively new. Because of this it is not usually regulated by the state which means that there may be many people who call themselves mediators but have little or no qualifications. There may be a heading in the phone book under Mediation. This can be a good place to begin. Call the mediators listed and ask them each to send you a resume prior to making any appointments to see them. This will tell you about the individual's professional qualifications. The local Attorney Bar Association also may have lists of names of people who do mediation. Mediators can be attorneys, family counselors, psychologists, social workers or other family therapists who have had additional training to qualify them as mediators. There may also be books in the library on mediation which will give you leads to local mediators. Most of these will list national mediation organizations which keep lists of their members. Membership in a professional organization is not a guarantee of competence but it certainly can be used as a guide to finding a competent person. The Academy of Family Mediators in Eugene, Oregon compiles an international list of family law mediators. Writing to this organization can be helpful.

Read the mediators' resumes well and talk to other professionals who know them. After you have seen some resumes, begin to make appointments with those mediators whom you feel are highly qualified. See several different mediators until you find someone with whom you feel comfortable and who you can trust. Once you have established a list of good mediators, tell your spouse so that the two of you can go to meet these people together. Go for an initial meeting to see if the chemistry is there and to see if the three of you can communicate well. Look for someone who is professional, trustworthy, experienced, and truthful, a good listener, and someone who seems to be able to grasp the full meaning of what you are trying to communicate and accomplish. Experience, background, educational qualifications, creativity, and good basic humanity are the critical measures which will predict possible success with the mediator. A knowledge of the laws of your state regarding divorce is also very important.

If the agenda of your mediation is to be concerned with working out a custody/visitation schedule, it is very important to focus on the children's needs during the mediation. Parents have told us many times that they want "only what is best for the children". However, this is not what they really mean. They really mean that they have decided what they think is best for the children and they want what they have decided. Mediation offers you an opportunity to seriously and thoughtfully consider the children in any settlement arrangement.

A competent and experienced mediator will place strong emphasis on how the parties handle the custody/visitation issues. The children cannot be used as pawns in the struggle between the parents. In order to be certain that the children's best interests are paramount; the mediator should have at least one private and confidential session with the children. In this manner the mediator can better understand the children's expressed needs and get a picture of their relationships with the parents. This experience demands that time be spent with the children. If this does not take place, the only information that is supplied comes from the parents who are angry, biased, and highly emotional and not usually thinking clearly.

There may be some situations in which mediation is not an appropriate activity. If one of the parties is a serious physical and verbal abuser who will make threats of harm and try to bully rather than cooperate, mediation will be of little value. There is no need to mediate if one spouse is going to ignore any agreements made or use the mediation sessions to harass the ex-partner. The mediator, upon seeing these styles, will most probably terminate the sessions. In other types of abuse cases such as physical/sexual or emotional abuse, mediation may not be proper. In this type of case it is far better to show the abuser that this will not be tolerated in any manner. Your attorney will file the necessary divorce papers and also be certain to include restraining orders for your protection. The court system can deal very effectively, swiftly and decisively with an offending spouse.

Any agreements which arise from mediation sessions are then finalized by the attorney so that the divorce can be obtained. However, agreements involving custody, visitation and financial support of the children are, in most states, always open and always have the potential for modification by the court at a point in the future. Spousal support may also continue to be modifiable by the court depending on the agreement and the laws of the state. Mediation of the case does not in any way preclude either party from going into court at a later date after a significant change in circumstances has taken place. Because of these factors, it is very important to know your local laws. In most states, the parties will be giving up their right to return to court regarding the division of property and debts. This is true for any settlement.

The reader is encouraged to give significant time and study to the mediation process and to make use of this excellent approach for problem solving. Any bright and creative alternative approach to the adversarial system is to be preferred. People who go through a divorce are severely emotionally drained, first by their decision to divorce and then by the court system. They usually do not realize how difficult the legal system has made it to get a divorce and to get the issues of finances and child custody settled. Anything that makes life easier and better for now and for the future is certainly worth considering. It is apparent that a positive working situation between the parties can be established, enhanced and cemented in by arriving at a settlement through mediation. If cooperation can take place prior to the divorce being final, there is a potential that it can continue throughout the years. When the parties demonstrate their trustworthiness through cooperation with each other, the children always have an easier time. Through this process they will receive fewer emotional scars from the divorce of their parents.

The mediation process also challenges the parties to take responsibility for their own individual part in the divorce as well as to see the process as a whole. Each party is able to see the relationship and the negative aspects which led to the divorce. In this manner each individual is able to break free of their own agenda. This is very important if the parties are truly interested in a divorce in current times. A divorce with sanity allows the parties to put aside petty differences and recognize that the primary concern must be what is best first for the children and then for the family as a whole. The individual needs of the parents must be sacrificed for the greater good.

CHAPTER 6
DIVORCE WITHOUT CHILDREN

There are numerous ways to handle a divorce when there are no children involved. Case histories can be utilized to demonstrate these alternatives in order to see: first, how different judges in different divorce courts will vary their approach to cases; and, secondly, to illustrate some of the different ways in which attorneys will deal with their divorce clients. By examning many different circumstances an individual can then decide what type of divorce s/he wishes to pursue and also the quality of the relationship that is desired with the ex-spouse. Divorce can provide a smooth transition into the single life style as well as an understanding of the role that the intense emotions will play in the divorce process. Divorce can also deteriorate into another way to vent anger and venom so that the goal is to exact vengeance, embarrass, and hurt the ex-spouse. Let us first look at circumstances not including children and then, in a following chapter we will carefully examine divorces which do include children.

The two major issues facing the divorcing couple with no children involve: the manner in which they will divide their property and debts; and whether either one of the couple will have to pay regular spousal support to the other.

Ralph and Janet had an eleven-year marriage. They had made a joint decision during their marriage not to have children. They found themselves growing apart the last few years until they had reached a point where they had little to say to each other with the exception of taking care of the administrative business of their daily lives. Janet decided that it was time for her to consider divorce because she had a growing awareness of deeper and deeper unhappiness. She was employed as an accountant for a large firm and Ralph was a manager of a local supermarket. Janet earned more money than Ralph, and almost all of their belongings had been accumulated during their eleven years together. They began talking about divorce because they both recognized that there was little life in their relationship and no real attraction anymore. They wisely decided to utilize the services of a marriage counselor and they attempted to put back some life into their relationship. After a six-month period of counseling it became evident that no matter how hard they tried nothing was going to change. They felt that it would be more comfortable to live separately and they did so. This was difficult for both parties initially but they soon settled in to a comfortable life style. They began to discuss a settlement because they respected each other and they knew that they did not wish to go to court to fight.

Ralph and Janet recognized that they needed to resolve the specific questions inherent in the legal issues of their divorce. They had to begin looking at how to divide their property in a manner which would be fair to both of them. They also had to determine whether or not spousal support would be paid from one to the other. They wisely decided that they wanted to spend the smallest amount of money they could on legal fees. They recognized that neither of them had any training in divorce law and certainly neither of them had ever been through a divorce before. They felt that they wanted to make this divorce as simple and as painless for both of them as possible. They also decided to do as much as they could without the benefit of attorneys. Ralph and Janet had numerous significant problems with which they would have to deal. They each had a pension through their jobs, they owned a home as community property, they had some community credit card debts, they had some stock investments and they also earned good salaries. These areas presented many problems and ordinarily they would require expert consultation.

The author does not recommend that a divorcing couple do their own divorce entirely unless they have almost no property or debts. The long term legal significance of a property settlement agreement can be great. It is therefore worth paying a competent attorney to prepare the papers. The costs can be held to a minimum if the couple can come to basic agreements on a settlement. If the couple owns little and has few debts, they can easily do their own divorce for the price of the filing papers. There are many practical, step-by-step guidebooks in the law library and in the local public library which are specifically designed to help this process and provide the necessary information.

In the case of Janet and Ralph, they are working toward an agreement. If they are able to resolve most of their issues fairly, then one of them can hire an attorney on an hourly basis to review the agreement, offer any necessary advice and prepare the necessary court paperwork. After this is accomplished, the other party could take the agreement to a second attorney of his/her choice for review as to whether or not this is a fair agreement. The same attorney cannot represent both parties which makes the second attorney's opinion very important.

The methods of mediation and collaboration have already been discussed and are gaining more and more acceptance with regard to working out the finances and property in a divorce agreement. Mediation services are neutral and the mediator does not represent either of the parties. The major goal is to arrive at an appropriate and fair agreement. Once this has been completed and a document prepared spelling out all of the aspects of the agreement, it should always be reviewed by independent attorneys and then put into legal form so that the divorce can be obtained. This is a relatively inexpensive procedure and assures both parties that all of their rights are being protected. Collaborative lawyers will work with the parties to stay out of court and come up with a fair and open agreement.

It is not unusual in divorce cases for one of the spouses to experience a significant delayed emotional response. This is most often a result of the individual not really dealing with the emotions that exist at the time of the break-up of the marriage. Initially the emotions are repressed but this defense wears thin and often gives way. Emotional reactions may occur at some later time when the parties begin to date and they run into each other or hear about each other's activities. At this point many emotions are felt and when they come to the surface they surprise the individual. The divorce may already have been finalized but if the party was not represented by an attorney, problems can arise. Anger and hurt may lead to seeking out an attorney who may advise that the settlement agreement can be overturned or nullified. Usually, this can only be done if it was unfair to this party and is within certain time limits. It is not worth taking the chance that this could happen and stimulate a full blown angry court battle. Therefore, the author strongly recommends that each spouse seek out the advice of an attorney even if they hire a mediation specialist in order to be certain that the agreement is a fair one. In this manner, neither spouse will feel that the other has had the opportunity to take advantage.

In the case under discussion, Janet heard about a mediation service in her city staffed by trained psychologists and attorneys. She contacted them and found out what the steps were with regard to working out agreements with Ralph. She was told that she should fashion an agenda. She was also told that the more areas that she and Ralph could agree on prior to coming in, the less time they would need to spend with the mediator and the less it would cost them. Janet and Ralph had a surge of increased motivation and they began to list their areas of concern and work out agreements. During the discussions they experienced many emotions and they realized that the divorce process is the most difficult thing they had experienced to date and certainly harder than they had anticipated. They attempted to resolve many different areas and they were successful to a point. At times emotions overwhelmed them and they had to stop until they saw the mediator. Even with these overwhelming feelings they were able to work out a basic agreement with regard to the division of their property and debts. Though Ralph may have been entitled to a small amount of spousal support, because Janet earned more money than he, they agreed that neither would pay the other support. The mediator helped them to see how they could offset this difference in earnings by agreeing on a slightly less equal distribution of the debts. In addition, Janet had been the primary wage earner while Ralph had gone to school to change careers so they felt that it would be unfair for her to have to pay any substantial support to Ralph. Janet and Ralph were able to work out a general framework for an agreement which they were able to refine when they went to mediation.

Because Ralph and Janet took advantage of the mediation service to help them with their divorce agreement, the process went very smoothly. They understood clearly that a court battle would prove nothing and that it would be costly both emotionally and financially. Though they both felt the emotions of the divorce, this process enabled them to be objective. They had decided that they would do all they could to not allow these emotions to cloud their ability to make a reasonable settlement. Because they chose to use the services of a professional mediator, they saved attorneys' fees and also supported their desire to work toward a compromise and to make a smooth transition out of their marriage and into a self-sufficient, single life. Both Janet and Ralph kept their divorce in perspective and recognized that it would be best for both of them to no longer be together. They felt the frustrations of failed expectations and they were experiencing intense pain and disappointment. However, they were able, through mediation, to find an avenue for settling their differences, *coming to agreements and moving on with their lives without allowing emotions to sabotage the process or their goals. Janet and Ralph had truly accepted the challenge to divorce with sanity as they took responsibility and worked with each other. They resolved their issues cooperatively and amicably.*

Had Ralph and Janet allowed emotions to take them over and dictate their behavior, they would have immediately run off to attorneys and they would have had even more difficulty coming to agreements. They would probably have ended up in court and had to go through a full-blown hearing. A judge would have divided up the property, allocated the debts, and made a decision as to whether one of them would receive spousal support. It is possible that Janet and Ralph may have wound up with the same or similar result that they came to through mediation. However, they would still have lost because by going to court they would have to pay significant legal fees as well as serious emotional costs. They also would have forced each other into the bitterness of the court action and this would have plagued them for many years to come. With the help of a mediator who has facilitated the process in a therapeutic manner, Janet and Ralph can remain on friendly terms and they never have to see the inside of a courtroom.

When your case is turned over to attorneys, especially if you want to have a fight with your spouse, then the attorneys will take their lead from you, get into the thick of it and fight it out, doing whatever they can to get you the best possible deal. The author has experienced numerous divorce cases where all sorts of smokescreens were raised to attempt to discredit one spouse and sway the judge. Attorneys and court can take your time and money and may ultimately get you little more than what you would have received if you had settled it yourself. It is simply not worth the harshness and emotional abuse which can result from the court experience. People take this foolish road because they are unable or unwilling to manage their emotions during a divorce and, often times, desire revenge or to punish the other spouse. They externalize the blame completely instead of taking responsibility for their part of the marriage break-up. When people refuse to seek professional help to mediate their divorce they often lose all perspective. They also seem to hire attorneys who either do not inform them properly or they refuse to listen to their attorney's advice.

It is interesting that even though we make our living being involved in court cases, we spend a great deal of time cautioning people to avoid court if possible. The legal system should be quite predictable, but it is not and therefore it is not worth giving up one's choices in life. However, we also do not ever mean to suggest that it is never appropriate to go to court. There are times when one party is completely intractable and unavailable and there are no other alternatives. Therefore, there are certainly appropriate instances when it is proper to hire an attorney to protect one's legal rights. Usually these are cases where one spouse wants to solve the property and support issues but the other spouse is interested only in venting anger, hurt and frustrations. In these situations, there is no other alternative but to hire an attorney. It is wise to explain to the attorney that a court fight is not really desired and it is wise to instruct the attorney to continue to work toward a fair settlement if possible. There are times when two bright and caring attorneys can transcend their clients' anger and work together. It is more often the case that when the attorney has an angry client, s/he is forced to adopt a strong adversarial position which definitely precludes any cooperative settlement.

It has been recommended here that the parties hire attorneys to help them resolve issues of distribution of property, debts and support. When there are assets as previously stated, attorneys can be very helpful in sorting things out for the couple. However, it is here that it becomes important for this couple to hire lawyers who are interested in helping them resolve their matters through non-adversarial means and by staying out of court. Choosing an attorney who supports this process will again save the couple stress and finances.

When a couple comes to their own settlement, they not only avoid the harshness of the court and the excess money they would spend, but they also get the opportunity to control how the property is divided. This is a very important consideration. For instance, the judge has no sentimental attachments to anything and can easily order liquidation of some special objects or property. By settling the case themselves, a couple can then decide who will get items of furniture, artwork, or other items. Both parties develop sentimental attachments to things that are acquired through the marriage. Sometimes an item is purchased because it has extra special appeal to one of the parties. Working out the settlement means that the parties can leave the marriage with a few of the things that were very important to them. There will always be disagreements as to some of the belongings but with a mediation or discussion process, compromises and sacrifices can be made so that items acquired in the marriage can be divided equitably. Neither partner will get everything they want but both parties have a better chance to get items that they are attached to if they settle between themselves. Different judges have different ways of handling the division of property and some of these ways may not be palatable to the divorcing couple. Judges generally do not enjoy dividing up a couple's property. They are usually of the opinion that the parties should be able to do this with the assistance of their attorneys. If you and your spouse do go to court, it is important to keep in mind that the judge will use some arbitrary but fair method of dividing up the property. Remember that when this happens the couple loses total control over this distribution. The author has seen judges simply take a list of the property and award items to each spouse based on equal values regardless of who wanted which item.

Frequently, one of the spouses will be earning a substantial amount more than the other. In these cases, it becomes clear that spousal support must be paid. Some people do not like the idea of having to pay spousal support and so they try to work out other arrangements.

For example, Sam and Ethel have been married for many years but have no children. Sam earns quite a bit more money each month than does Ethel. He has stated that he does not want to pay spousal support because he is angry that Ethel is the one who wants the divorce. It is very probable that if they went to a court hearing, Ethel would be awarded a significant amount of spousal support. Since they both wanted to avoid a court hearing they tried to find some common ground on which they could settle their case. One possible alternative is for Sam to give to Ethel an unequally large share of the marital assets in exchange for her agreement not to take spousal support. If Sam were to quitclaim to Ethel enough income producing property, then this could be considered to be a reasonable and proper settlement. In this manner they have the opportunity to tailor their agreement to take into account Sam's emotional needs and to still be fair to Ethel's financial needs.

There are an unlimited number of creative solutions that a couple committed to a peaceful resolution of their divorce can utilize. Those couples who are unable to come to agreements on their own are usually too angry, too hurt and too disappointed to want to settle their differences. Their need for vengeance becomes primary and therefore, it outweighs their ability to think clearly. In fact, there are times when these negative and hostile feelings sometimes take people over entirely. Their lives become dedicated to destruction. There are also those cases that present rare legal or factual issues or in which exceptionally large amounts of assets may be at stake. These cases often tend to be highly publicized but they occur only rarely. In these divorces, the couples will sometimes choose to risk not coming to a compromise agreement in favor of the possible opportunity they might have to gain a large amount of the assets. Often the reason these cases receive so much publicity is that one of the spouses is unwilling to work toward an agreement and so s/he hopes that publicity will sway sentiment in his/her favor. At times the spouse who is being left behind is so upset that this party refuses to reach an agreement. It is more important to this person to punish the other spouse regardless of the cost. The goal is to make life miserable for the other spouse as a punishment for leaving. The goal of gaining a fair or reasonable settlement is not even considered. Of course, this type of hostility eventually turns itself in and attacks the very person who is expressing it.

Ruth and Herman had been married for many years and had never wanted to have children. As Ruth approached forty, she began to feel a strong urge to be a mother. Herman had no desire to have children, and, in fact, he truly despised children. As Ruth began to express her needs, Herman forthrightly reminded her numerous times that when they were married they had discussed this and agreed not to bring children into the world. Ruth was now changing her feelings on this issue and Herman was getting angrier and angrier at her. The disagreements and agitation continued to escalate on a daily basis until it was clear that the marriage was no longer tenable. Ruth was feeling so strong on this issue that she gave Herman a strong ultimatum stating that she was prepared to divorce him if he did not consent to her having a child and cooperate with her needs. Herman, who had been the primary wage earner in the marriage, became furious. He could not understand Ruth's point of view since they had both been so certain about not having children. Ruth, seeing Herman's obstinance and anger, moved out of the family home and promptly filed for divorce. Later she approached Herman about working together to settle their divorce but he was so angry that he did not want to speak to Ruth. Instead, Herman hired an attorney known in the local area as a 'barracuda'. They are also sometimes known as 'sharks'. He specifically instructed this attorney to make certain that Ruth received the least possible amount of support and the least amount of property from the marriage.

In this circumstance Ruth is left with no alternative but to hire her own barracuda attorney and fight back. Of course, when she did find an attorney, he was anything but a barracuda and she instructed her attorney to try and settle the case with Herman's attorney. However, Herman was so dedicated to destruction that he refused to even attempt any negotiations. As a result, the Ruth and Herman case snowballed and took on a life of its own. They became embroiled in a bitter court fight that used up an enormous amount of time and many thousands of dollars from the community assets. The net result of course, was that Herman would clearly have fared better if he could have set aside his anger and agreed to a settlement. In the court battle Ruth received more than she was willing to accept in a settlement.

    This dreadful situation happened to Ruth and Herman because of anger. Herman felt that Ruth had defrauded him, violated their spoken agreement not to have children and he was very angry about Ruth changing her mind. Herman decided to dedicate himself to punishing Ruth. However, he never was able to accomplish his goal. Instead, he accomplished a large attorney expense and a division of property and support order for Ruth which was not in Herman's favor.

    This is not an unusual vignette when relationships deteriorate to this point. Herman had the opportunity to settle when Ruth made her offer. Since Ruth was feeling somewhat guilty for being the cause of so much upsetness, her offer was quite generous to Herman. Herman could not see past his anger and pain which controlled his actions and brought him and his attorney into court to do battle to the death.

    Our experience in Herman-Ruth situations is that neither party can really come out as a winner. The bitter battles only engender more lasting hostility. The couple continues to undercut each other and this does not settle anything. The attorneys who command large salaries do well when the anger levels are this high between the parties. Some clients believe that winning means making life miserable for the other spouse. However, in the long run this is not at all true. For these reasons, it is imperative to look at the relationship between emotions and the divorce itself. It is very difficult to keep emotions in perspective when one is feeling the pain of divorce. However, people who desire to settle their case peacefully have a healthier outlook and invariably do better than they would have if they had gone to court. Rather than seek out a barracuda to do battle, it is far better to seek out an attorney, mediator or a therapist who will help you to keep the divorce in perspective. Only in this way can the parties get through the issues with the least amount of pain. In this way they can move ahead with greater success. Divorcing spouses have the choice to allow their emotions to control them or to realize the dangers inherent in this process. It is far better to seek out professional help to avoid the expression of anger through a protracted and expensive court battle. This does no one any good and only serves to further damage the individuals. In order to more effectively move forward in life, the settlement option is by far the best choice.

CHAPTER 7
DIVORCE WITH CHILDREN

The issues around child custody and parental visitation have the potential to seriously compound the problems of divorce. It is important to recognize as we have stated in a previous chapter, that there may be numerous alternative avenues which can be utilized, offering very different ways of reacting in these circumstances. Divorces in which all of the children in the family are over the age of eighteen and have completed high school (and therefore considered to be adults in most states), are really treated in the same manner as divorces in which there are no minor dependent children. In the circumstance with children who have reached their age of majority, the issues of child support and custody are actually non-existent. Some rare exceptions to this rule can arise if the children have severe handicaps or if they are mentally or physically challenged, or if they have special ongoing medical or psychological needs which the parents must supply. In these situations one must specifically seek out consultation with an attorney who can provide the information and the procedures which are dictated by the particular state in which the parties reside. Throughout this chapter, for the purposes of the illustrations concerning divorce when there are children in the home, we will utilize situations in which the children are dependent minors.

In divorcing families with minor children there are three major issues which must now be added to the normal issues of divorce. These issues are the problems inherent in child support, child custody and visitation of the children by the non primary custodial parent. In fact, today, the term visitation is being used less and less and the term custodial plan is being used more because it is offensive to many people to be categorized as "visiting" their child.

Natalie and Tom had been married for fourteen years and were now in the process of separating. There are two children from this marriage, ages nine and six. Natalie and Tom owned their home. Tom was employed as a branch manager with the government and Natalie managed a woman's clothing store in the local mall. Tom earned three times as much as Natalie and they were both paid on a monthly basis. Natalie always performed the traditional roles of taking the primary responsibility for the care of the home and the care and raising of the children. At the time of the separation Tom left the home and he moved into his own apartment. They talked and felt that they may not need two attorneys. They decided that Natalie would be the one to seek out and consult with an attorney about the procedures in the divorce proceedings. They both sadly agreed that it was time to separate and they each felt hurt and disappointed that this marriage would end in a divorce. Every young married couple believes that their marriage will last forever and Natalie and Tom were no exception. They agreed to try to avoid a nasty divorce and instead, to work things out themselves with the help of a mediator, and then an attorney to file the court papers. The children, a boy and a girl, were to remain in the family home living with Natalie, their mother. In addition, Natalie's widowed mother would also move in to help with the children.

However, Tom was a very involved father and he wanted to spend as much time with his children as he possibly could. He wanted to continue to participate in their regular activities and especially their school programs. Tom and Natalie arranged a visitation schedule which would guarantee that Tom would see the children one evening each week for dinner, as well as every other weekend from Friday after school to Monday morning when he would take them back to school. In addition, he would have half of the holidays, the entire Easter vacation, half of the summer, and he would also be able to speak to them by phone on a daily basis at specified times.

The most important question, and, in fact, that first question that a divorcing couple must ask is how to arrange a custodial schedule for the children. They are dedicated to their children and they need to maintain their focus on their children's needs. The second question involves how money will be apportioned. The amount of support is not only based on the relative incomes of the couple, but also on the amount of time the children will spend with each parent. If Tom only saw the children for just the two weekends each month, then his expenses for the children would be less and therefore, Natalie's expenses for the children would be expanded. These expenses encompass the daily living expenses such as food, gasoline expended to shuttle the children to their various activities, baby-sitting fees, and various other child care costs. Fixed expenses such as ongoing monthly mortgage payments do not ordinarily change no matter how often the children are in the home or out of the home. If Tom has the children with him for a longer period of time, it is appropriate that this should have an impact on the amount of child support he pays to Natalie. In a circumstance where both spouses make approximately the same income, and they share custody of the children almost equally, then in most cases it is probable that no child support would be paid from one to the other. In this case the parents would share equally in any expenses incurred by the children. These will include items such as: medical insurance; medical co-pay expenses over and above the amount covered by insurance; educational expenses; clothing; dental and vision expenses; etc. Each parent would most likely pay these costs when they occur and then share them with the other parent at a specified time.

Prior to figuring the support issues, the custodial schedule must be agreed upon. This is often very difficult to accomplish because of the emotions inherent in the divorce, the ages of the children, the differing work schedules of the parents, the change in living conditions, and numerous other practical issues which may impinge and need to be made part of the equation.

One of the most characteristic patterns noted by the author is the use of the children to get back at the other spouse because of the hurt and disappointment of the divorce. Our experience is that if a couple is truly interested in assuring that the children continue to have a good relationship with both of them, they are able to overcome, compromise, discuss, and resolve all of these practical issues. In circumstances where one parent wants to insidiously block the visitations, or poison the children against the other parent, these practical problems escalate into continuous mini-wars. Many excuses are found to keep the other parent from spending more time with the children. When the children do go to see the other parent, the antagonistic parent may pull some passive-aggressive behaviors which are consciously designed to prejudice the children. An example of this is when the father comes to take the children the mother holds them very tight, kisses them forty times and says things like, "Have a good time at Daddy's, if you can", or, "I know you will have fun, I will pray for you". These are just some of the many classic passive-aggressive statements we have heard. This behavior is completely inappropriate. It is designed only to sabotage the relationship between children and parent and it must be stopped immediately!

Assume that Natalie and Tom never got along well and that Natalie forced Tom out of the house and filed immediately for a divorce. She refused to speak to Tom to attempt any workout of their problems and she further blocked him from speaking to the children on the telephone. When he called she would have the telephone answering machine on and then not be responsive to his calls. When she did pick up the phone, she would tell Tom that the children were outside playing, eating, sleeping, at a

*friend's home or otherwise unavailable to him. She also made
it difficult for Tom to have any meaningful visitation with the
children. When he would come to see them for his assigned and
agreed-upon weekend, she would be gone and he would wait
on the doorstep for hours with no sign of the children. Because
of these overtly hostile and destructive behaviors, Tom is now
forced to hire an attorney, go into court, and request that the
judge order Natalie to allow him to see the children on a specific
and regularly set schedule from which Natalie would not be able
to deviate. Natalie, as a way of striking back and leveraging Tom,
now demands exorbitant amounts of child support and requests
the court allow her to move from the area with the children.*

*As an extra-added feature, Natalie, through her voluminous
tears, states in court that she believes that there might have been
some sexual acting out between Tom and the children. When this
accusation is made, it is as if the world stands still. The local child
protective service office must now be contacted and more often
than not the parent against whom the accusations are made will
not see the children for three to six months. It is apparent how
this can result in a disturbance of the child-parent relationship.
This eleventh hour molest charge is often utilized in these types
of cases and once spoken it must be thoroughly and completely
investigated and evaluated. This sometimes backfires as the
accusing parent may also lose custody of the child for a period of
time. Sometimes these children are placed in a shelter or foster
situation until the accusations can be sorted out and investigated.
If nothing is found, the accusing parent is then suspect in every
area and frequently loses out in custody. At this point both parties
are in a full-blown court battle fighting over the children and using
them against each other.*

This type of bitter and hostile divorce is all too common. It is costly financially and emotionally and the parents generally forget that they are supposed to be looking at what is good for the children. Instead, they are guided by their own hurt, disappointment and anxieties. Failed expectations in a marriage inevitably lead to frustration, passive and direct aggression, anxieties, disappointment and blame. One of the effective ways that divorcing couples use to get back at each other when they do not live up to their expectations in the marriage, is to use lack of access to the children as punishment. In most families it is the children who are most important to both of the parties. When one or both are forced to have prolonged separations from the children, this becomes a very difficult problem for everyone to handle. Oftentimes the children are completely unaware and in the dark as to why they cannot see one of their parents. Their only conclusion is that they did something wrong or that they are bad and this is why the parent won't come. They feel that they are being punished but they have no concept of the struggle between their parents. We have seen these children grow up and we have seen them as they begin to grasp the understanding about what happened. Their inclination is to punish the accusatory parent for denying them a relationship. This may result in delinquent behavior or simply leaving to live with the parent they have not seen for many years.

The author has had a great deal of experience with men who have moved from their large homes into a small apartment. When this takes place the children are always left behind with the ex-spouse and the separation is very painful for all concerned. This separation pain exists even when the parent is able to spend a great deal of time with the children because it is not an ongoing daily living situation. When the parent moves out, that parent not only becomes separated from the ex-spouse but also from the children. Even in those situations where both parties know that the marriage cannot be saved, and both know that the divorce is inevitable, this separation is extremely difficult. The parent who remains with the children may attempt to compensate for the loss of the spouse by becoming overly involved and overly protective of the children. When that person tries to interfere with the children going to the other parent for extended time, the over protectiveness becomes harmful and negative to the children.

It is very often the case that the angry parent who remains with the children wants to vent frustrations on the other parent. By doing this, the parent knows that the result will be painful to the ex-spouse.

Satisfaction then comes with this knowledge because it fulfills the desire for revenge. It is very sad to note that in most circumstances it is the mother who is left at home with the children and therefore, it is she who tends to play these anger games.

Helena, a woman in her forties with three children, consulted with the author concerning her divorce process. She stated that she was so upset with her husband that she was doing everything she could to consciously interfere with his visitation with the children. She knew that the only way she could effectively get back at him for leaving was to make certain that he suffered as much as possible and paid a dear price before he was able to see the children. She admitted that in actuality he had always been a good father and that the children loved him. She knew that what she was doing was not only bad for her husband but also for the children. She also had insight into the fact that if she continued, her behavior would get more and more obvious. She knew that she too would at some point begin to feel that fall-out of the anger as everyone started to focus in on her behavior. She said that even though she knew all this, she could not help herself. She wanted her husband to suffer, suffer and suffer some more because she felt so unhappy and miserable about the divorce.

In this illustration we see that even though Helena was aware of her behavior, it was as if she was addicted because she also felt that she could not or did not want to stop herself. Most people do not even comprehend that they are behaving in this manner. They use everything that they can to interfere with the other parent's time with the children and they make poor excuses and rationalizations for their behavior. It is very important for people who do this to gain as much insight as possible and take positive action based on that insight. In this manner it is hoped that they can learn to change their behavior and cooperate with the other parent in assuring that the children get enough good quality time with both parents. In Helena's case she was counseled to make immediate changes in her behavior or she would suffer the consequences in court. She did not heed this advice and she stomped out of the office determined to leave her ex-husband a bloody pulp by the side of the road. She easily found an attorney who would take her husband to the Supreme Court if he had to so that she could continue her negative behavior. As predicted, when her husband brought out the facts in court and supported these facts with witnesses, Helena's bad behavior was punished by the judge. She lost custody of her children and was forced to see them only during specific visitation times. Naturally this exposure to this negative behavior hurt all concerned.

Another client, Donald, earned a very high six-figure salary each year. He left his wife and two children behind and moved into a large, very comfortable condominium not far from the family home. His wife was the one who wanted the divorce and he was very angry at her. She had a part-time job which she enjoyed a great deal and it allowed her to earn enough money for extras. The family had always enjoyed a very high standard of living and Donald was now not sending any money for support. His wife and children very desperately required financial support from Donald. Initially, Donald, in his anger, stated that he had told his wife that he did not intend to give her any money. He also told her that he was planning on forcing her to leave the home. He threatened her by saying that he would then take the children and she could "live on the streets". He felt that she deserved this type of treatment because she was the one who wanted the divorce. Donald did not feel that the divorce was a necessary step at all. He had little or no understanding of their problems and his typical approach was to try and smooth things over, rationalize and deny that problems existed.

Donald was always a stubborn man in all respects and it took a great deal of time to help him to see that it was his own pain and disappointment that was leading him to say and do such irresponsible behaviors. With insight he saw that he was only hurting his children by trying to make their mother unhappy. He was also interfering in his own relationship with them because all of his freethinking time was spent devising ways to get back at his wife. If he had brought this attitude into court, a judge would have very little patience with him. Unfortunately, this is a relatively typical case. Most husbands still earn larger incomes than their wives. Because of this they often tend to actively manipulate and leverage their wives by threatening and also by actually withholding financial support.

Many divorcing people try to manipulate each other. They do not realize that the actions they take to interfere with their children's relationship with their spouse, also adversely affects their own relationship with the children. They also do not realize that this most certainly affects their chances for realizing their goal of achieving custody. One of the fastest ways to lose custody of the children is to prevent their other parent from seeing them. Unless there is a special reason such as child abuse or sexual molestation, this should never be done. The laws are very clear in that they will always support the parent who is cooperative and who goes the extra mile to insure that the children have a good ongoing relationship with both parents.

Trying to be as detached as possible at the time of separation is helpful so that parents can do what is best for the children rather than what satisfies their own revenge motives. At all times the parents should keep in mind the fact that they have a strong moral obligation to their children to encourage relationships with the other parent. When we can look at the anxieties inherent in separation and divorce from the children's point of view, we recognize that it is an extremely threatening circumstance. It is best for them to keep their relationships with both parents as solid and normal as possible to help them to get through the difficulties.

It is certainly obvious how interfering with the relationship with the other parent can be detrimental to both parents' relationship with the children. A parent can easily sabotage the relationship between the children and the other parent. This can be accomplished in the most obvious way of limiting the amount of time the children spend with the parent. It can also be done by not including or informing the other parent of important activities which occur in the children's lives such as: medical appointments; sports events; and school activities such as plays, open house and teacher conferences. This will interfere with the non primary custodial parent participating in the important parts of the children's lives. Another negative way of undermining the relationship between the children and the other parent is to speak negatively of that parent to the children. Attempting to poison the children against a parent will inevitably come back to haunt the manipulating parent at some time in the future. Children grow up and they begin to see the truths because they are then able to view the actual circumstances with more objectivity. Negative parental behavior will backfire at some time. When the children realize that mom or dad is not really that bad a person, they wonder why all the negative things were said. Frequently, the next step that the children take is to reject the manipulative parent and want to live with the other parent to get distance from the negative atmosphere.

When parents attempt to manipulate or brainwash they may be creating highly negative situations for the children later on in life. These manipulative situations can take their toll in affecting the children's relationships with peers as well as with authority figures and with their own spouses when they grow up. The parent who has fostered this negative position must take the responsibility for bringing about these traumas due to their own selfishness. Unfortunately, most parents who believe in this manner are not willing to assume the moral high ground by taking responsibility for their actions. Instead, they prefer to take the low road and place all blame on their ex-spouse.

Emily and Dan had three children, ages nine, seven and four. They had been married eleven years when they agreed to separate and divorce. Their agreement to separate was reached not through a mutual feeling but through a massive fight in which each loudly blamed the other for the failures in their marriage. Their intense anger dictated many revenge-seeking behaviors from both of them. Dan moved into a small house nearby while Emily remained in the family home with the children. Dan wanted to spend as much time with the children as he could and also remain involved in their sports and school activities. Dan worked full-time while Emily worked part-time. The two older children were in school while the youngest was in day-care for three days each week.

    Almost immediately after their separation, Dan and Emily began doing things which were consciously or unconsciously designed to irritate the other. First, Dan sold an extra car they had. He kept the money and never discussed with Emily his intentions with regard to the money. Of course, he did all of these car transactions without any consultation with Emily. Emily retaliated by running up excessive charges on their credit cards for things that were not really necessary. They both complained to the children about how incompetent and mean the other parent was acting. Emily did not inform Dan of activities or conferences for the children at school. She rationalized it to herself by stating that if he was really that interested and he loved them that much, he would find out for himself. As a result, Dan missed seeing his seven year old in a school play, the child's first program. Dan retaliated by buying the children many toys and taking them to many amusements each time he saw them. Emily became quite upset because she could not compete with Dan financially and she felt that Dan was giving her very little toward the support of the children. She then found reasons not to let the children spend time with Dan, and started telling the children that he had been a very poor father all during the time they had been married. None of these statements were true but in her zeal to retaliate effectively, this did not seem to matter to Emily at all.

    Soon, Emily and Dan escalated to the next level which included attorneys. They each hired attorneys who were aggressive, highly adversarial and very strong. The attorneys sabotaged each other by refusing to return each other's phone calls and soon they were acting just like their clients. Emily and Dan found themselves in court numerous times over small events and they were spending very large amounts of money. They each decided to fight for custody of the children since each was now thoroughly convinced that the other parent was certainly the worst parent in the entire universe. When you say this and think it long enough it becomes believable. Because of the custody *fight, a judge decided to appoint a psychologist to evaluate the children and both parents and make a recommendation to the court as to which parent should have primary custody. Both attorneys counseled their clients that they should have their own expert since the court appointed psychologist might not bring in a supportive report. They each hired their own psychologists and of course they were not permitted to speak to each other or to share data. In fact, they did not even know of each other's existence in this case. Everyone was kept in the dark. This meant that the parents and children would most likely repeat the same tests at least twice and perhaps even three times over. Now the parents were actively arranging for their children to be traumatized even more by having to go through the entire divorce with three different professionals. By hiring their own experts, Dan and Emily each believed that their attorneys had recommended someone who would be favorable to them and who would definitely say in court what they wanted the expert to say. Dan's psychologist was not going to be permitted to see Emily, and, Emily's psychologist was not going to be permitted to see Dan. While the court appointed psychologist was completing the evaluation of the whole family, with no knowledge of the other two experts on the case, the judge, who also had no knowledge of the other experts, made temporary orders. These orders covered a visitation and support schedule for Emily and Dan to follow.*

As the time for the hearing drew closer, the parties instructed their attorneys to begin to talk about settlement because it became apparent that there would be no winner in this matter. Emily said that she would agree to Dan spending more time with the children if she received the bulk of the marital property. Dan said that he would rescind his fight for custody if Emily would agree to a minimum amount of support. Dan had moved out of the family home taking essentially none of the household items or furniture. He decided that he had made an error in leaving so fast and he now wanted some of the home items. Emily agreed that he could have some of the household items if he would give up his fight for custody. Dan made the point that most of the things he would want were items which were not even used by Emily. She did not care and told her attorney to tell him that he would get nothing from the house unless he gave up his fight for custody. However, Dan did not want to give up his custody battle, not because he wanted the children so much, but because he enjoyed the fact that Emily was so threatened by the idea that she might lose the children. Most of these discussions were taking place through the attorneys, though sometimes Emily and Dan would try to talk to each other. Most of these talks ended in hostile, bitter arguments and replays of the original arguments with nothing taking place and no positive forward movement.

The process of using the division of marital property and financial support as leverage is very common. This has become a usual means of trying to acquire what is desired with regard to custody/visitation agreements. These trade-offs can also be made in negotiating the division of property and the payment of support, whether that be spousal support or child support. Most couples try to use their negotiations in an effort to come to some relatively fair agreement. Other couples attempt to control the division of property, financial support, and the custody and visitation questions by dictating to the other party what they will or will not accept. This attitude is specifically designed to create conflict. The party adopting these attitudes is saying that this will be the way that all of the decisions will be made. It is always intimidating when one spouse tells the other that he or she owns all of the control in the issue. The other spouse will always resent this position and a full-blown conflict will follow. These attitudes are used either consciously or unconsciously for the purpose of punishing the other spouse and not for the purpose of negotiating a settlement. Settlements are not negotiated by buying or selling the children or through force and brute strength. Instead, they are successfully negotiated by exposing all of the information and by agreeing to make compromises while also looking for new avenues of agreement.

Dan and Emily were telling the children how rotten the other parent was. As a result, the children became confused, angry and they began talking to their parents less and less. They did not wish to be caught in the middle and they did not want to say anything which might offend either parent or start either parent insulting the absent parent. The parents' only interest was to get back at each other. As they continued, the children's performance in school began to deteriorate. They went from being social, extroverted people to being quiet, withdrawn and introverted. Behavior in school became worse and each parent reported these changes to their attorney, blaming the other parent for the problems. Dan's attorney, feeling that Emily was trying to control the children, immediately went into court and asked the judge to appoint an additional attorney, paid for by Emily, whose sole job would be to represent the children. This is not an atypical request and in more and more cases we are seeing attorneys specifically appointed to represent the rights and best interests of the children. The judge agreed in this matter with the proviso that the attorney's fees be split between both parties. He appointed an attorney for the children, recognizing at this time that neither parent seemed to have the best interests of the children at heart. The judge saw that each attorney was arguing the case for the client while no one was speaking for the rights of the children.

The attorney appointed for them, met with the children privately to get to know them, see how they were doing and see what they wanted. It was very difficult for the children to communicate with the attorney because they were fearful of the possible repercussions. They felt that if they said anything at all, it would get back to one or both of their parents and they would then have to listen to more complaints, hostility and bitterness. It took the attorney several meetings with these children in order to build rapport and help them to see that their thoughts and feelings were safe. Finally, they began to feel confident and believe that he would not tell either of their parents the things that they said. The two older children complained because they did not understand why they had to see three psychologists, or even one psychologist. The children felt that something must be wrong with them or else their parents would not be sending them to so many psychologists. They felt that they must be the cause of their parents' problems with each other because the parents continuously complained to the children. They began to dislike both of their parents and they began to dislike being with both parents because they no longer wanted to hear the negative statements and complaints. As a result, the children became even more quiet, withdrawn and their poor performance in school escalated. They confided in their attorney that things were getting worse for them. The attorney noted that as the hearing date got closer, the parents started to put even more pressure on them. The children were the targets of intense manipulative persuasion by both mother and father.

Unfortunately, this type of case is becoming more and more common. It serves to demonstrate how the divorcing couple can express their emotional behavior and anger. They are motivated by their needs for revenge and by their own selfishness. Emily and Dan were really into the struggle completely but they are novices compared to some. They cared much more about their own personal battle and each decided that s/he wanted to be the winner no matter what the cost. Of course, the children represented the prize. They no longer had any insight or understanding into the children's needs. They had each successfully convinced themselves that if it was good for them it would be good for the children. The author has seen many divorcing couples behave in this manner and worse. When the children are used as pawns by the parents, the game loses its rules and life deteriorates. The only attention the children receive is when they are either being bribed or brainwashed. The children typically act out, misbehave in school, become involved with the wrong crowd, steal, shoplift, use drugs and we see the effects of insidious parental abuse. The children do this because they are crying to be heard and noticed. They try to cause trouble under the unconscious assumption that this might be the very thing which would bring their parents together. They often feel that their parents will heal their wounds and stop their battles if they have to focus on solving the children's legal or behavioral or school problems. The tragedy is that the more the children act out, the more the parents blame each other and the more they continue to ignore the needs of the children.

Emily and Dan continued to escalate the issues. When judges appoint an attorney for the children they tend to lean heavily on this attorney's opinions. They feel that this person can truly give the most honest and accurate recommendation as to what is truly in the children's best interests. The attorneys for the parents represent their clients with the contract that they will do all they can to win the case for their client. The attorney for the children has only their needs to represent and no others. The attorneys for the parents were certainly aware that the judge would be seriously listening to the recommendations of the attorney for the children.

As might be predicted, the psychologists hired by Emily and Dan recommended custody for their individual clients. They did this in violation of their own ethical standards because they had not seen the opposite parent. The court appointed psychologist stated that if the parents could not get along better and stop saying and doing negative and hostile things to the children, then perhaps the children should be placed in the home of a relative or in a foster home. The attorney for the children told the other attorneys that unless Emily and Dan stopped involving the children in their fighting, he would recommend that neither parent have custody. He stated that the damage was too severe and that they all required psychotherapy in order to stop the toxicity in this situation. Emily and Dan knew that their children would be welcomed and treated very well in other relatives' homes. They both became afraid that they would lose their children and this brought some insight and clearer thinking into the picture. They began discussing a settlement with the assistance of the three attorneys. Soon a reasonable and effective custody/ visitation arrangement was agreed upon. This kept the children living primarily with Emily but spending a great deal of productive and quality time with Dan. Dan also agreed to pay a reasonable amount of financial support to Emily after some verbal armtwisting. They were both lectured extensively by the judge and told that they were no longer to speak ill of the other parent in front of the children. The judge let them know very directly that he could change the arrangement and bring the family back into court on his own motion at any time. He said that he would appoint a Special Master to oversee the issues and that there would be a review of the existing custody/visitation arrangement every three months to see if Emily and Dan were behaving. He ordered conjoint counseling for the parents to work out their anger and divorce feelings. Dan and Emily eventually went to a full hearing to let the judge decide their property division. Unfortunately, they were still at war, but they had listened carefully to the judge and they had removed the children from the heart of the battle.

This example demonstrates how divorcing couples use the children against each other and lump this together with the other issues of financial support and property division. The reasons for the existence of this type of behavior generally lie in the intense pain, anxiety and blame coming from each of the parents. Their perceptions of everything are distorted by this anger and it causes them to inadvertently harm their children. This harm can exist for so long and be so severe that it may even be irreparable.

The author has seen this process repeated numerous times. We attempt to counsel clients not to retort if they hear that their spouse has said something mean about them. By rising above the anger and not playing the game, they preserve their individual positive relationship with their children. Children love their parents and they do not want to hear or believe negative things about them. If one parent continues to try and poison the children and the other parent refuses to do the same, the children will usually turn against the parent doing the negative talking. Children do not want to be placed in the middle of their parents' fights. As stated, If parents do this, they will eventually pay a dear price as the children act out their frustrations and emotional disturbance.

An important aspect of an effective custody evaluation approach is the psychological evaluation. This is often critical in correctly discerning what would be best for the children.

THE PSYCHOLOGICAL EVALUATION RE: CHILD CUSTODY

Not long ago courts only recognized psychiatric testimony which was normally utilized in criminal matters. When issues of custody became more refined, and judges wanted to know more, psychiatrists would often testify as to where a child would fare best. However, psychiatrists utilize an interview and occasionally they use some computerized testing services. Psychiatrists also utilize many brief paper and pencil questionnaires which have neither statistical validity nor reliability. They are not educated as to test construction or statistical analyses of tests. In addition, psychiatrists are specifically not licensed to administer, score and interpret psychological tests. When it became apparent that psychologists could offer more than psychiatrists in custody matters the psychologists fought for more recognition in the courts. In the early nineteen eighties states began to make changes and accepted psychologists. The California legislature passed a law indicating that psychologists could no longer be discriminated against and a new field opened up to aid in the protection of children of divorce.

When an especially acrimonious divorce appears on the scene, the mediation or conciliation arm of the court will often recommend for a psychological evaluation. Most judges appreciate this recommendation because they do not have to make a ruling on little or no information. Instead they can now have the benefit of a great deal of information from a psychological standpoint which will help the judge to feel that his ruling has more validity.

Most often, when the parties have attorneys, one of two different systems may be utilized. First, the attorneys make recommendations to each other of psychologists they know whose work they respect. The attorneys and clients then decide on one psychologist to do the complete evaluation and they stipulate to the report coming in as evidence subject to cross examination. The second method of selecting a psychologist involves the judge offering to both parties a list of three psychologists. The parties then must agree on one of the psychologists from this referral list. There are some judges who have their favorite psychologists and they simply offer one name and say that this is the person they are appointing to complete the evaluation. No matter which selection system is used, most times the parties split the bill between them subject to the judge apportioning it at a later time.

There are as many psychological evaluation methods as there are evaluators. Each evaluator has his/her favorite tests and procedures. Generally, the evaluator will first read all of the pleadings and declarations, depositions, and any other material that the attorneys wish to present. Often this can be an enormous mound of paper especially in cases that have dragged on for a long time. The evaluator not only reads all of the material but s/he also contacts any therapists, teachers, previous evaluators, mediators, relatives, etc. If there are any other relatives that live in the same home as the children, these people are also evaluated. In addition, if the parties have new spouses or live-ins, they are also evaluated. It becomes obvious that this project can absorb a great deal of time and energy. Some evaluators will take months to accomplish the evaluation. Although they may be very thorough and highly professional, taking this long is not appropriate. The reason for this is that over a period of months there can be many changes in the family and the evaluation will be stale as soon as it comes out. It is far better to find a psychologist who can complete the entire family evaluation with the same thoroughness and professionalism within a period of approximately one month.

Once the psychologist has familiarized him/herself with the case, the parties are then evaluated. Normally, each of the adults will first be seen individually for an extensive interview. We recommend the DTACC (Diamond Technique for the Assessment of Child Custody). This is a comprehensive interview which offers to the evaluator a great deal of highly pertinent information. First, a complete mental status interview is accomplished as well as the intensive custody oriented interview. The clinical interview and mental status exam is an in-depth procedure aimed at understanding the patient's ability to effectively utilize social judgment, insight, and awareness. Questions are asked to document historical information, ability to handle problems of living, capacity for making good associations, progression of thought processes, emotionality, decision-making and relationship ability. This leads to the more intensive custody oriented interview and should take approximately two hours to complete. There are literally hundreds of psychological tests that can be utilized. Most evaluators will do the Minnesota Multiphasic Personality Inventory. This is a 567 question, true-false, forced choice personality test. The test measures areas of: hypochondriasis; depression; hysteria; schizophrenia; characterological psychopathology; sexual role-identification; tension; anxiety; emotional energy level; and introversion-extroversion. Additional content scales include: anxieties; fears; obsessiveness; depression; health concerns; bizarre mentation; anger; cynicism; anti-social practices; type A behavior; low self-esteem; social discomfort; family problems; work interference; and negative treatment indicators. It is a valid test and it is scored statistically. Although this test is specific to the measurement of psychopathology, it does not directly offer information as to parenting ability. However, if the protocol indicates a great deal of pathology, it certainly follows that these problems will affect an individual's ability to parent effectively. The MMPI takes approximately one and one-half hours to complete. There are other inventories which can also be utilized. These are also tests of pathology, some of them tied to the Diagnostic and Statistical Manual of Psychiatric Nomenclature. Frequently, the evaluator will administer the Rorschach Technique commonly referred to as the ink blot test. This test offers the patient an ambiguous and unstructured set of stimuli. The patient must integrate these stimuli and respond in a specified fashion with free associations and then with answers to an inquiry. The test is scored and interpreted both objectively and subjectively. It often consumes a great deal of time in administration, scoring and interpretation. There are also numerous tests which attempt to predict parent-child interactions, propensity for sexual abuse, and whether there are any special tendencies which might lead to violence against spouse or children. Many of these tests are paper and pencil questionnaires. Although their validity may be in question, they have excellent data to offer in the hands of a skilled evaluator. Parents might also be administered tests of intelligence if this is an issue. The most used test to measure a wide range of intellectual skills is the Wechsler Adult Intelligence Scale. If there is a suggestion of excessive alcohol use or organicity due to alcohol and drug use, the evaluator might utilize the Bender Visual-Motor Gestalt Test, or The Wechsler Memory Scale, or numerous other tests specifically designed for evaluating alcoholism and its residuals. The Bender is especially useful. This test demonstrates whether an individual can integrate visual stimuli into a meaningful whole and reproduce them through motoric action in drawings. The individual's ability to effectively integrate a given stimulus constellation demonstrates central nervous system integrity.

Oftentimes the evaluator will present questionnaires such as The Symptom Checklist to define both the physical and psychological symptoms that an individual may experience. A Sentence Completion Test has value to look into the quality of both familial and interpersonal relationships. Projective Drawings can have value as well as other traditional projective tests such as the Thematic Apperception Test. This test offers the patient highly unstructured but non-ambiguous pictures of individuals in social situations. The patient must construct stories covering the elements of: what is happening in the pictures, how the people are thinking and feeling, what led up to the circumstance in the picture, and how the story ends and what becomes of the characters. This is analyzed subjectively with regard to content and how the individual is able to construct interpersonal relationships.

After the adults are individually evaluated, they will often be seen with the children. Some evaluators feel that seeing the children with the parents offers a small snapshot of how they respond to each other, the parenting skills and their general relationship. Other evaluators feel that even the worst of all parents can sustain an hour of play with their children and so the parent-child interaction session is of little or no value. It is our position that this is not the most useful of data gathering situations, but it can lead to interesting information. During this session the parent and child or children are asked to complete a cooperative mandatory task and a cooperative voluntary task. The interaction, social skills, parenting skills, creativity, disciplining skills and comfort levels of the parent and child are observed and evaluated. Therefore, we like to see the children in different sessions on different days with each of the parents, stepparents or parent surrogates.

The children are then evaluated individually. Once again there is a wide range of approaches to the children. Some evaluators feel that observations are more important that testing. Unfortunately most evaluators do not know how to successfully evaluate children so they will skip it if they can get away with it. These are the evaluators who also send out the adult testing to computerized services and receive a report. They do none of the testing work which unfortunately turns their report in a sociological study rather than a true psychological evaluation.

When the children are tested they should receive a well rounded approach to data gathering. This should always begin with a very complete interview-rapport building hour to put the child at ease and also to document relationships and mental status. The items one should discern through the mental status exam include: general physical appearance and hygiene; facial expressions; range of emotion; general affect; speech; cooperativeness; clarity of thought; manipulation; social skills; body movements; humor and sarcasm; intellect, insight and judgment skills; orientation in three spheres; information recall, small detail awareness; compulsivity; planning skills; creativity; small and large muscle skills; imagination; anger; consistency; ability to express feelings; sensitivity to self and others; awareness of the custody issue; sex-role assignment; truth-telling; test cooperation; independence; activity level; affection skills; personal depth; hand, eye and foot preference; eye tracking and accommodation; and gait. This may appear as a great deal of information but a skilled psychologist can discern these matters very quickly. A complete evaluation should also include a test of intelligence such as The Peabody Picture Vocabulary Test. This is a non-verbal test of intelligence for children. It is based on the child's hearing and sight vocabulary. The child is asked to select pictures depicting various aspects of the environment and concepts frequently utilized. This is a power rather than a speed test, well standardized, and it offers an excellent estimate of I.Q., mental age, and percentile and stanine rankings. Once we know how intelligent and sophisticated the child is with regard to understanding his/her environment, we can offer tests of organicity and projective tests. The Bender is usually administered along with the Rorschach and the Projective Drawings. If the evaluator is skilled and competent, the children will almost always enjoy the testing sessions.

Once the adults have been tested and the children have been tested, and the parent child interactions have been noted, and all the reading and contacting of collateral contacts has been accomplished, the evaluator is ready to write the report. In addition to outlining all of the data, the evaluator has to pull together the needs of the children and the strengths and weaknesses of the parents in terms of their ability to meet those needs. The evaluator then concludes his/her report with a specific recommendation and submits the original of the report directly to the judge. Copies of the report also go to both attorneys and sometimes to the court mediator. The parents do not get a copy of the report directly from the evaluator unless they are in pro per (representing themselves). At times it may be quite hurtful for the parents to read the report. The initial contract they make indicates that the evaluator has the right to gather any information s/he believes to be pertinent. In addition, the evaluator may discuss with each party, what the other party says. The concept of privilege (keeping information private and confidential) falls by the wayside in a custody evaluation. Attorneys make the error of immediately copying everything to their clients without evaluating whether this could be destructive.

When the judge has the psychological evaluation report there are a number of approaches. First, the attorneys can counsel their clients that it looks like the judge will go along with the recommendation of the evaluator. Therefore, the clients would be wise to accept the recommendations and see how they work prior to coming back to court. Second, if the level of acrimony stays high, there will be a win-lose situation. One of the parties will feel that s/he has won and the other will feel that s/he has lost. The 'loser' can bring in another psychologist at the hearing to try to counter the court appointed evaluator's conclusions. In addition, the 'loser's' attorney may recommend that the evaluator be cross examined in the hope that some cracks in the recommendations can be brought out. They have the right to cross examine, but once again the judge will not be happy with a long, drawn out, protracted court session that will accomplish nothing. The 'loser' runs the risk of losing even more. Of course, it would be far more appropriate for the attorneys to get together and see how they can implement the recommendations of the evaluator. If these recommendations are valid and the parents follow through, then the children will thrive. This is what the judge is counting on since s/he feels that the added psychological material can dictate a far more sophisticated and appropriate response. Therefore, it should be apparent to the parties and the attorneys that the judge will support his/her expert and urge the parties to utilize the results of all this work.

     As divorcing parents, awareness of the traumas that may be visited on the children is most critical. Getting caught up in the emotions of the divorce is not unusual and it requires the services of a therapist to help sort out feelings. Frequently divorce counseling for the parents is very appropriate and timely and very healthy for the children. The use of the children in bargaining the financial support and property settlement issues by manipulating the custody/visitation schedules is inappropriate. The selfish needs and vindictiveness of the parents should not be placed above the true needs of the children. We have seen this negative manipulation far too often. Divorcing parents must be encouraged to put aside their own anger, fear, disappointment and anxieties especially with regard to their children. Only in this way can these parents accept the challenge and responsibility of a healthy divorce. The optimum position would be for the whole family unit to be taken into consideration and not just the selfish and individual needs of one or the other.

CHAPTER 8
MAINTAINING A WORKING RELATIONSHIP

Our experience clearly demonstrates that the better the divorcing couple gets along during their divorce, the easier will be their future relationship. The adults will eventually adjust and function better as will the children. However, there are many ex-spouses who seem to believe that they have a mission to keep the battles raging long after the divorce is final. They undercut each other constantly, use the children for purposes of manipulation, and always play a one-upsmanship game. This may offer some devious pleasure to one or both of the ex-spouses, but it is always unproductive, agitating to all concerned and ultimately very destructive. If the spouses are not regularly fighting, but instead, are working together to solve problems and deal with the children consistently, life is much easier for all concerned. In order to maintain this type of relationship one has to exert energy, work for it and be dedicated toward not acting out even when angry. Many divorced couples sabotage each other and regularly appear in court fighting about things or about children. They say rude and discourteous things about each other and they denigrate each other's life style. Couples who do get along after the divorce have made an effort to put aside their angers and petty differences. They work and make a specific effort to keep their relationship on a cooperative and comfortable level. This is the ideal. Some might ask why they should want to maintain a good working relationship with an ex-spouse if they have no children. Most of the time couples with no children go their separate ways and have little or no contact after they divorce. However, they are psychologically healthier people when the break-up and settlement is agreeable to both parties and they have worked through the feelings of fear, anger and disappointment. Underlying the anger there is still some residual of mutual caring and this should be nurtured. Divorcing couples may have many reasons to remain in contact. Perhaps the husband or wife has a child or children from a previous marriage who has bonded with the stepparent. This bonding may be strong enough for the divorced couple to remain in contact so that the stepparent can continue to have a meaningful relationship with the child. This is especially true if the marriage was of long duration and the stepparent was highly instrumental in the raising of the child. Our experience has demonstrated that this is not an uncommon occurrence. We have frequently noted that in families with stepparents, the bond with the child may be even more significant if the biological mother or father has not maintained regular contact with that child. It is important for the divorcing couple to have the insight and recognition that this connection between stepparent and child exists and cannot be summarily broken just because of a divorce. If they do have this awareness, they will allow the relationship to continue to thrive and flourish. This will certainly be beneficial to all concerned: parent, stepparent and child.

    The child benefits because any relationship with a significant and caring adult is positive. The child will be able to maintain the relationship and therefore not be forced to suffer the full impact of the trauma of separation and total loss. The stepparent continues to benefit because this permits an ongoing opportunity to love, maintain the contact and show the child that love rather than abandonment survives. The natural parent benefits as well. The parent is seen as encouraging and fostering the bond with the stepparent. This helps the child not to have resentment for the divorce toward the natural parent. The divorcing couple recognizes that, in many ways, the impact of this divorce on the child is the same as if this child were a natural product of this marriage. Divorce court will often not establish visitation between the child and stepparent because the child is not legally a result of this union. However, in California there are now code sections that do allow the judge to order visitation to a stepparent. Even if the court is not able to order these visitations due to individual state laws, this should not stop the divorcing couple from recognizing the important effect the divorce and separation from a stepparent has on a child. This assumes of course, that the divorcing couple had a reasonably healthy relationship in which there was no physical or emotional abuse of each other or the child. In unhealthy relationships between couples where there is long-term abuse, the child will be thrilled and happy to see the couple breaking up. In these cases, it is doubtful that the child will even want to see the stepparent, if the stepparent has been the abusing parent. If there was serious physical, emotional or sexual abuse it would be unhealthy for the child to maintain a relationship with the abusing parent.

Another significant reason for maintaining a working relationship and contact with an ex-spouse lies in the fact they may still share property or business in common. Even though they may wish to detach, it may not be economically feasible at the time of the divorce. As an example, if the couple had rental property during the marriage, and if the real estate market is not favorable to sell, they may have to keep the property in both names. Taxes, investment possibilities, maximizing the value of property or wishing to maintain some property in both names for the children are all good reasons for continuing to have a positive working relationship. We have noted numerous situations where the two parties were complete failures at being marriage partners but they were excellent business partners because their business skills complimented each other very well. At times they may try to sell the family business and need to maintain their working relationship in order to keep it profitable so that it will be an attractive sell. In this type of situation it is to the benefit of both parties to get along and maintain a good working relationship so that they can realize the maximum from their investment. If the business is exceptionally successful, there are couples who decide to keep it and operate it together even long after the divorce has become final.

It is apparent that there can be many good reasons for wanting to maintain a good relationship with an ex-spouse. In order to accomplish this, it will require not only hard work but also an open mind. It is wise to investigate why many couples cannot maintain a working relationship after the divorce so that their bad techniques will not be repeated. People who fail at having a cordial relationship after the divorce do so because they are still unwilling to let go of the angers and the resentments inherent in the old relationship. They remain hurt, disappointed, blaming or afraid. They believe that because the marriage was not successful, these feelings are the fault of the ex-spouse. Effort must be made to see the reality of the situation, that is, that the parties are no longer married and therefore, no longer responsible to each other and no longer involved in each other's life. It is of no benefit to continue to carry around the negative feelings and to continue to heap blame on the ex-spouse. If this is done, it simply keeps the two people stuck in the same unproductive and angry rut. They maintain a poor relationship with each other and they are stuck in feelings and emotional experiences which are constantly debilitating. Effort needs to be expended so that the parties can accept the reality of the circumstance in which they now find themselves. By so doing, they will move on to new relationships rather than dwelling on the past negative experiences. When the past negatives are the central focus of one's life, it keeps one from having competent and healthy relationships in the future. Far too much energy is expended in negative thinking and acting, and nothing is left for the much-needed healing process to take place.

Fred and Karen were married for nine years before Fred decided that he wanted a divorce. They had no children but they did have some property including a family home. Karen did not want to end the marriage and she was highly traditional and very dependent on Fred. He wanted to leave because he was feeling suffocated by Karen's intense dependent needs. Karen was highly threatened when Fred broke the news to her. Her immediate feeling was that she felt that she could not get along in the world without him to guide her and make her decisions. Karen began to feel even more anxiety than usual which resulted in her clinging to Fred and the marriage with even more fervor. Of course this served to drive Fred further away until the marriage was entirely broken and the divorce was inevitable. The couple went through a fairly simple divorce since they did not have a great deal of property and they both had good jobs which provided roughly similar incomes.

    Fred and Karen had very little interpersonal contact after their official separation because Karen was very angry that Fred had actually gone through with the divorce. She was dedicated to her own private fantasy that he would back out at the last minute. Karen was pathologically stubborn in maintaining her denial throughout the process. At this point she could not even bear to talk to Fred or to see him. She was very hurt, afraid and angry because she was being forced, very much against her will, to confront the truth that her marriage was ending. She was certain that it was all Fred's fault and her anger grew from the fact that she could do nothing but accept Fred's position that he did not want to try anymore. Karen spent much of her time wringing her hands, lamenting her fate and blaming Fred for her pain. She also started to criticize herself for not having been able to maintain the marriage with Fred and she now found herself to be continuously depressed and miserable without this relationship. Because Karen is faced with the finality of this divorce, she now has the opportunity to carefully examine why she continues to be so hurt, angry, and afraid even after the marriage has terminated. Although friends have attempted interventions and urged her to get psychological help, she refused. Consultation with a *competent, licensed psychotherapist is critical for Karen at this point. An examination leading to insight would help Karen to see why she was initially involved with Fred and why she so easily became highly dependent on the relationship. This would then lead her to realize the unhealthy parts of the relationship which she would not like to repeat again in the future. She would then be able to effectively investigate her own dependent tendencies so that she would not have to repeat these needs and activities with anyone else. This insight has an additional benefit because it could also lead Karen to a better post-divorce relationship with Fred, or if she chose no relationship at all.*

It is obvious that Karen needs to have the opportunity to make her own decisions based on her own psychological growth and understanding rather than being blocked by a need to hold on to a bad relationship at any cost. Holding on through ignorance and lack of understanding of the feelings and emotionality will always cause bitterness and pain. This is the approach that Karen took. She chose to deny and stay blind to the reasons she initially married Fred and the reasons for the divorce from Fred. Because of this style, Karen will probably carry this same negative psychological baggage and agitated dependent behavior into her next relationship. This will mean that in time she will have the same difficulties once again. Karen's opportunity to grow as a person is there for her to take and is a perfect example of what we have been referring to as the challenge of self responsibility. This is the point at which Karen needs to demonstrate responsibility and accentuate her own personal psychological growth.

Accepting the reality and the individual responsibility for the divorce requires one to examine one's own behavior toward the ex-spouse after the divorce has taken place. Continuing the vendetta or the anger, hurt and fear is the hallmark of divorce anxiety. This is the symptom that is most dangerous when one courts it and embraces the negative thinking. Everyone who goes through a separation and divorce experiences hurt, pain and disappointment even if the divorce is wanted. These are normal experiences which one cannot avoid. However, the problem exists when the divorce is over and time has gone by but the anger, hurt, and disappointment have not dissipated and they are still in evidence. If one has not fully accepted the divorce at that point, and the emotions are still debilitating and fearful, counseling with a licensed professional mental health worker is in order. In fact, our court system would run far smoother and our families would be far healthier if every divorcing couple had to have mandatory psychological treatment during the course of their breakup. Currently the courts have recognized the value of mediation with regard to child custody and visitation. Hopefully, the value of a psychotherapeutic approach will also be recognized so that many parents and children can be spared the agitation and turmoil they currently experience.

If one member of the couple is ready to be friendly and one is still being angry and rude, a cooperative relationship may be very difficult. The healthier party has to be highly flexible, look past the anger of the other party and recognize that for some people it is more difficult to move on with life. A non-reactive and calm approach is best in this situation. This attitude encompasses an understanding of why the ex-spouse is adopting these negative attitudes, and a refusal to become caught up in the hostility and negativity. Reacting with the incompetent interpersonal techniques of the old marriage will lead to continued disaster.

Jack and Jill were married for seven years before they divorced. They had no children but they owned a very large, expensive home and a thriving business together. Jill wanted the divorce and Jack did not. They were able to work out a settlement agreement that was favorable to both of them so that they could stay far away from a court struggle. They put the family home that they had both occupied up for sale in hopes that they could spilt the equity, giving each enough cash to get a fresh start.

Jill wanted to keep the business together because they were good, cooperative business partners. She noted though, that whenever they were at work at the same time, Jack would be subtly mean, rude and nasty to her. He would say cutting things and not take her views into consideration when important business decisions had to be made. Jack was still very angry about the divorce. Jill decided that she would not respond to Jack's barbs and negative comments. She made the assumption that if she did nothing to continue to provoke him, he would eventually get over his anger. She recognized that either consciously or unconsciously, Jack wanted to get into a fight and prove that he was right about everything. She verbalized for him what she felt he was doing and she did not allow herself to be drawn into any verbal sparring matches. She also made it clear that they would not be getting back together so they had better accept the reality of the divorce and get down to the business of running a successful, money-making enterprise. Jill waited, but even after several months Jack was still being mean and trying to provoke her. Jill confronted Jack carefully and told him that if he did not get some counseling to help him to see what he was doing to her, they would be forced to liquidate the business. She made it clear that if he did not change she could not continue to work with him. Unfortunately, Jack did not want to stop being angry and he did not want to make any changes. He refused to seek help and continued to be angry and rude toward Jill. She did eventually force the sale of the business and after this there was no further contact between the two of them.

    In this case, Jill was able to move on with her life and accept the reality of the divorce without placing the blame on Jack. It is true that she was the one who wanted the divorce so she had done a great deal of thinking and examining of her feelings prior to making her announcement. Even with this, it was very difficult for Jill because she had always hoped and planned for her marriage to last forever. Jack was never able to accept the reality of the divorce or the part that he played in the problems they had. He continued to externalize all blame and blame Jill for everything. He could not take any of the responsibility for himself. This produced the offensive behavior of rudeness to Jill and it ultimately caused the sale of the business that had once earned them both a very handsome living. Jack courted these negative feelings and would not let go. With these negative attitudes he could never hope to be able to enter into a healthy relationship with another woman. Jack chose not to be responsible for his role in the divorce and therefore could not hope to experience any personal growth as a result. We have all known people who could not let go of their relationship with their ex-spouse. They make this the central focus of their lives going over and over all of the "injustices" that they believe took place. They constantly feel sorry for themselves while blaming their ex-spouse for all of their misery. These people are not moving forward in their lives because these negative attitudes stop any forward emotional growth. This type of attitude can be avoided if there is insight into how completely non-productive it is. The object is to become aware of self-needs through the divorce so that the negative attitudes are not perpetuated. If the anger, hurt and resentment are allowed to fester, the future will be affected and other relationships will be doomed to disaster. Psychotherapy is most important during these difficult days.

If there are children involved in the divorce it becomes especially crucial to try and maintain a good working relationship with an ex-spouse. In order to insure that the children continue to have the opportunity to be nurtured by both parents, they have to see their parents in as positive a light as possible. Ideally, we would want them to see their parents as supportive and respectful of each other even though they choose to no longer live with each other. If not, they will believe that they too can be divorced by their parents and left behind. A good working relationship does not mean that the parties have to fall in love again, go out to dinner and spend a lot of time with each other. Instead, it just means that the parties are aware, courteous, civil and respectful of each other. They have to work at being considerate when they meet and they have to refrain from saying rude and negative things about the other parent in the presence of the children. They also have to be certain that other relatives do not pick up the gauntlet and say negative and hostile things when the children are around. This is done because of concern, love and dealing with the best interests of the children. The parents want to deal with their emotionality and not continue to carry around the negative feelings. The process of getting revenge is not a priority. It is also not a priority to punish the ex-spouse for not being the husband or wife that one thought they should have been during the marriage.

Parents looking at the divorce from the child's point of view will learn a great deal. They need to ask themselves a number of very important questions:

1. How is my child handling the divorce from a behavioral point of view?
2. What does my child want to happen between the parents?
3. What are my child's feelings toward each parent?
4. How does my child react when one of the parents slips and says something negative about the other parent?
5. Are my child's feelings and well being important enough for me to seriously look at my actions with regard to my ex-spouse?

Rarely do we find children that approve of dissolution between their parents. Most children just want things maintained. Even in a bad family situation, they usually still want to have two parents. Of course in an abusive situation the children will be sufficiently angry so that they will support the divorce. This is an extremely difficult time for them because they are either largely ignored or used for leverage in the tug-o-war between their parents. Even in those cases in which the home life is so difficult for the children that they want their parents to live separately, this is still a very difficult time. Far too few divorcing couples allow themselves to really see their divorce through the eyes of their children. Far too many parents use their children to get back at their ex-spouse.

The author has noted that many parents cannot get past their need to utilize denial as a major mechanism. They pretend that everything is just fine between them because they feel that this is the best way to deal with and hopefully avoid any potential psychological upset in the children. However, children are almost never fooled. They can tell when there are problems and when their parents are being less than completely truthful with them. A divorce is a very important decision that always affects the children as well. It has been demonstrated in our experience as well as in the literature that even very young children want to be kept informed so that they can more fully understand what is happening in their home environment. Within their own level of understanding, the child should be told what is happening and given some basic, but truthful reasons as to why things are taking place in this particular manner. It is also a time when the child needs to know that s/he is still loved by both parents and that this will never change. The parents have to understand that until they were separated, the child would have freely seen each parent every day. Parents who have limited awareness and do not recognize this will try to keep the children from the other parent. This only serves to hurt the children, deny them information, and upset them for long periods of time. It may also serve to turn the child against the offending parent.

Looking in from the outside we see people doing some amazingly stupid things. We often wonder why some divorced parents who would not hesitate to die for their children, suddenly have so little information concerning their children's needs. They play these dangerous games of using the children against the ex-spouse and their behavior is blatantly destructive to all concerned. Their anger and disappointment becomes the controlling factor so that all other valuable information is clouded out of the picture. The parents lose their perspective and just continue to blame their ex-spouse for all of their problems. Unconsciously they see that there is one very effective way to get revenge for the pain that the ex-spouse has caused them. This is to turn the children against this parent by saying rude, nasty, and horrible things to the children about the other parent. If this is done in conjunction with interfering with visitation with the other parent, it will undoubtedly be very effective. The children and the money are the most important aspects of the ties that still bind a divorced couple. This presents us with the ready-made formula that we see so often. The mother who has primary custody of the children gets back at her ex-husband by interfering with his ability to visit with the children. The husband then has the ability to get back at the wife by not paying her the child or spousal support to which she is entitled, and he ignores his ongoing responsibility as a father.

The real effect of this behavior is negative, hostile and can lead to irreparable damage to the children. First, it makes a working relationship with an ex-spouse an impossibility. Second, it keeps the children in the middle of the battle between the two spouses. The children become alienated from the parent who is manipulating and sometimes alienated from both parents. They know that their mother and father are not terrible people and they wonder why they keep hearing these comments from them. It is interesting to consider that the parents were once married to each other, conceived the children together and parented them well. Now that they are divorced they begin to say that the other person is incompetent to be a parent and was never any good from the beginning. This is not an appropriate way to look at an ex-spouse and even more inappropriate to say to the children. In fact, when the parents are both successful in letting go of each other, they have the opportunity to become more caring parents after the divorce than they were during the marriage.

It is clear that any behavior that does not encourage a healthy relationship between the children and the parents can only be negative for all concerned. Children learn how to effectively deal with the opposite sex by using their parents as role models for behavior. When parents are modeling this type of hostile behavior on a continuous basis, it will undoubtedly interfere with the child's future relationships. Many adults carry emotional wounds inflicted on them by their hostile and angry parents. The more awareness divorcing parents have of this process, the less likely they will do this negative behavior because they will not want to risk scarring their own children.

Bob and Norma had been married fourteen years when Norma decided that it was time to separate and divorce. They had fought a lot during their marriage but both of them had a difficult time emotionally with the separation and divorce. They had three children: a twelve-year-old boy, and two girls, ages nine and seven. They had married when Bob was twenty-one and Norma was eighteen. Bob spent the entire marriage working to support the family while Norma took care of the home and the children. They were involved in a complex, long term, very neurotic love-hate relationship that gave neither of them much pleasure. They had bonded together in a negative fashion and neither of them actually realized this either during the marriage or at the time of the divorce. It was this negative, dependent bonding pattern that caused them to have so many fights and arguments during the marriage. When it finally became unbearable, Norma announced that she wanted to end the marriage. There was not much property to divide and financial support would be paid according to a computerized court schedule. Norma had found a good job to help with the finances and the only issue left to fight about was the custody/visitation plan concerning the children. Norma felt that the children should continue to live with her and that Bob should see them only when she felt that it was convenient for her to allow this. Bob wanted to spend more time with his son specifically, but was happy with the arrangement that the children would live with Norma. However, in line with his hostility and the negative relationship that they had, he did not tell her what he really wanted. Instead, he told her that he wanted primary physical custody of all three children because he knew full well that this would upset her a great deal. He also rubbed it in further by telling her that if he did not get custody, he would quit his job and not pay support, no matter what the court ordered.

Both of these people were so angry at each other that the only thing they could see was their own anger and hostility. They had a poor relationship and throughout their marriage, neither had lived up to the other's expectations. They were set for the battle so that they could get back at each other one final time for having a bad marriage. Neither would accept any responsibility for their role in the marriage since they enjoyed blaming the other for all of the problems. Neither paid any attention to what would be in the best interests of the children. Norma and Bob had a bitter and hard fought custody battle involving many *psychological experts and attorneys. The judge decided that their son would be spending approximately half of his time with each parent, while the girls would live primarily with their mother and have a liberal visitation schedule of approximately one-third of their time with Bob.*

This is a plan that they could have agreed upon through mediation without ever having gone to court. However, since it was ordered by the court, both parents fought it and continued to fight each other. From the beginning of this court ordered arrangement, neither parent followed the rules. Both demonstrated behavior which was blatantly in contempt of the order. They would pick the children up early or late, drop them off early or late, and not be available at all sometimes when the other parent was to come for the children. Bob held out his child support payments and made them only after the District Attorney threatened him with jail. Even then he would pay late and he would typically write NSF checks until they had to go back to court once again so that the judge could order him to pay Norma with a cashier's check each month.

Each parent would continually say horrible things about the other to the children. Bob and Norma would grill the children getting them to report on what the other parent was doing, who s/he was dating and what s/he was saying. Bob would stalk Norma and watch her for hours to see what she was doing. They would have telephone conversations in front of the children regarding school or health problems that would inevitably wind up in screaming, cursing matches. They would find small things to do to each other to cause continued irritation. For example, Bob would not tell Norma about an important sports activity involving their son. Each forbade the children from calling the other parent while in their home and refused to put telephone calls through to the children from the other parent. This was consciously done by both parties even though it was clearly a violation of the court order. They would sign the children up for extra-curricular activities that interfered with the other parent's time. Then when

*the parent did not want to, or could not take the children to these
activities, that parent became the ogre. Norma "forgot" to tell
Bob that one of the girls was injured at school and broke her
leg. These games between the parents continued as they fed
each others' hostilities. They had no awareness of how stupid
they were and how bad they looked to others including their own
children.*

Many children can transcend their parent's stupidity but others get caught up in it and become highly disturbed because of the anger and double messages that come through. Norma and Bob's children tried to ignore their parents' behavior in hopes that it would stop. However, it continued to get worse. The children had good relationships with both parents during the marriage even though the marriage was so poor. Now, they were unable to control their lives and they felt that they were under constant verbal bombardment from both parents. As time wore on and the parents perpetuated their battles, they kept dragging each other into court. As each decision was made, it would exacerbate the angers and the effects were beginning to show in the behavior of the children. Their grades became so poor because of the excessive stress they felt, that the youngest child was kept back a grade in school. Their son became involved with drug users and was arrested for theft and brought before the juvenile delinquency court. The older daughter began to torment her younger sister unmercifully for no reason. Norma and Bob continued to blame each other for this behavior of their children, and, without knowing it, they were both correct. Rather than deal with the problems and deal with their angers, they used these issues to continue to fuel the fires of their past relationship.

An inexperienced reader may think that this example is excessively extreme. Unfortunately, it is more the norm than the extreme. Many divorced couples behave in this manner. Others engage in some of these behaviors but not all of these patterns. Clearly, in these situations, the children are caught in battles existing between their parents. Neither parent truly cares about the effect that their behavior has on their children. Their only concern is to inflict further agony on the ex-spouse. In all cases this is negative with regard to the emotional health of the children. The divorced couple, instead of trying to keep a positive working relationship so the children can thrive, have kept a negative working relationship which is designed to produce emotional disturbance in the children.

It is interesting to see how many couples refuse to let go. Many would rather continue a bad relationship after the divorce than have no relationship at all. These people continue unhealthy contact with their spouse even when they are made aware of the pain they cause. In fact, their goal is often to create this pain and they are being successful. They are cemented in the disappointment, anger, and hurt of the relationship. They cannot get past these feelings and they do not want to detach from their ex-spouse since this is how they express their angers. They unconsciously fear losing the connection and the only way they can relate is to hurt each other. Oftentimes these people become involved in the relationship and the marriage for unhealthy reasons. Since they never resolved the reasons that caused them to come together, they continue to relate to each other based on these old patterns even after the divorce. Counseling would be very helpful. However, since each person believes that the other is responsible and they do not see themselves as the source of the problem, it is an uphill struggle. The odds of getting these parties into a voluntary therapeutic circumstance are very poor.

Brenda and Jerry were married for seventeen years and they have two girls, ages thirteen and eleven. Their marriage had been difficult for each of them, and, over the last several years, they had purposely become more involved in their jobs than in each other. They were able to agree on a settlement of their property and debts very quickly. The girls, realizing that their parents were splitting up, announced to them that they preferred to spend the bulk of their time with their mother and have regular visitation with their father. Brenda and Jerry accepted their needs as expressed. They were highly responsive and they arranged a mutually agreeable visitation schedule. Both were upset, hurt and angry about the divorce because neither spouse could live up to the unrealistic expectations of the other. Each blamed the other more than themselves for the breakup of the marriage but they each became involved in their own individual psychotherapy so that they could understand their feelings. Because the girls had always related well to both parents, Brenda and Jerry recognized the importance of encouraging these relationships. Though they were upset with each other, they made a verbal agreement not to say negative things about each other to the children. They also agreed to set aside some consistent time when they could speak to each other about any problems that might come up between them that involved the girls. They additionally agreed not to do this when the girls might be available to hear their conversations. They encouraged their daughters to talk with them about their feelings. They also encouraged the girls to spend as much time with their other parent as they desired, regardless of the specifics of the written custody/visitation agreement.

As a result of the active, cooperative posture demonstrated by Brenda and Jerry, they were eventually able to pick up their own individual responsibility for the failure in their marriage. This process then allowed them to resolve their own pain and disappointment. The girls were able to continue to grow in an emotionally positive manner because both parents' homes provided them with equal love, warmth and support. It wasn't long before Brenda and Jerry could actually be comfortable and friendly toward each other and freely discuss their children. They also moved forward so that each was eventually able to become involved in other opposite-sex healthy relationships which did not pose a threat to the other party or to the girls. Brenda and Jerry did it correctly even though initially, they were both very unhappy about the divorce. Their story clearly offers us an excellent example of how a divorced couple with children can still work through their pain and anger while maintaining an effective working relationship. They are not any brighter then most or even more insightful than most. However, they stayed tuned in to their children and stayed aware of the needs their children *had that they, as parents, were the only ones who could satisfy. Without doubt, this not only benefits the adult parties but also the children. Couples, who truly value their children's mental health, make efforts to respect each other and interact with each other in a positive manner.*

These examples make it clear why it is so important to maintain a positive working relationship with an ex-spouse. If there is an abundance of hurt and anger and the parties blame each other constantly, this is a clue that they are very much in need of psychological counseling, either individual or conjoint. Arguments provoke even more anxiety and the parties become even more opinionated and angry at the whole world. These are the issues which must be attended to and resolved. This creates psychological disturbance and agitation in the children that can be long lasting and destructive. Power plays never have winners or losers. Power plays are used solely for the purpose of perpetuating the reasons for the divorce.

The divorcing parties require counseling so that they can be reminded of the needs of the children and so that they can keep these needs uppermost in their minds. They have to stay aware of how their children could be affected by the divorce and the new changes that they will have to go through. Considering the needs of the children will allow them to have continuing and healthy relationships with both parents. If the parents keep each other informed of interesting and important events with regard to the children, they will foster effective communication and they will present themselves as excellent role models for the children to emulate.

Parents should be aware that they can communicate with each other through a number of modalities. They should be encouraged not only to speak with each other but also to write, fax, and e-mail each other. In this manner the material can be consulted numerous times and allows the parent time to think and consider the issues. We encourage the parents to keep a log book for communication about the children. This logbook consists of a notebook/journal in which the parents communicate with each other with regard to their children and their needs. Parents write questions, information, things to watch for, activity schedules, medication schedules, and positive statements. They do not write complaints about each other to each other. They are to keep uppermost in their minds that the logbook is a specific vehicle for the process of communicating about their children only. The custodial parent writes a minimum of one line per day per child to alert the other parent as to how the child fared that day. In this manner, the parties will have a living history of their children's activities. The journal always stays with the children and is exchanged at the visitation times to enhance effective communication.

      The divorcing parents always need to remember that they must focus on their children's future. If this is the case they will keep aware that their children cannot be happy unless they are able to develop the skills that are necessary to develop and maintain healthy relationships with peers and adults alike. Parents who do this act in a responsible and competent fashion, thereby successfully accepting the challenge of a Divorce with Sanity.

CHAPTER 9
DIVORCE IN A NEW AGE

Anyone who has ever spent any time observing the activities in divorce court is well aware of how completely unresponsive divorce court can be to the needs of individuals and families. We might ask ourselves why we even bother with this archaic system when it apparently does not help very much. Instead, it often winds up hindering the healing process and hurting families. It is unfortunate that many people that we know, including our children, may at one time in the future have to face a divorce. It would be far more psychologically healthy for the divorce system to adapt a kinder and more sensitive approach so that the people we love would not be hurt.

Although each state has its own set of divorce laws, the general procedures and philosophies are fairly similar and rooted in ancient canon doctrine. Every state utilizes the same basic principle which is to purposely pit the husband and wife against each other. The wife hires her attorney who is sworn to present her case in a manner which will result in her winning everything she wants for herself. The husband hires his attorney who is also sworn to present his case so that he wins everything he wants as well. Each member of the couple looks at the other party as an adversary and an enemy. The attorneys look at each other as adversaries and they do their best to sway the judge by supplying her or him with their spin on the information as well as the appropriate dramatics. The attorneys argue, dance around the truth, establish new truths, re-write history and do their best to convince the judge within the bounds of the rules the court establishes. The judge has the job of making the final decision as to which of the attorneys wins, if either of them in fact do, and how much of the assets each of the parties will win or lose. This system forces the parties to work against each other and not with each other. Chances for settlement are slim once they go to court armed with all of their possible arguments. Each attorney and client plan strategy and plan how they can sway the court to get the best possible deal. Husband and wife are dragged along in this process and this occurs when they are at their lowest point emotionally and psychologically. This is apparent to anyone who has ever been divorced or has ever seen a couple struggling over their divorce in court. The theme is win, win, and win, and of course, payback. If someone wins then the other party will lose, lose, and lose. This is a healthy concept when one goes to a basketball game but not when one is dealing with very sensitive and complex interpersonal, parent-child and child-environment relationships.

    At the time the parties decide to separate, they are in the midst of enormous emotional turmoil. Breaking up any long-term relationship is difficult, but a marriage is far more difficult to resolve than anything else. It is a more difficult circumstance when the couple has children and property. When they had said holy vows to stay together, they remember that at one time, they were very much in love. Now, when they are each at their most fragile and vulnerable state, when they are afraid and angry, when they are hurt and disappointed, they are supposed to be making important decisions regarding children, money, marital property and debts. The court makes certain to pit the two spouses against each other at the time when they are most likely to blame their spouse for the failure of the marriage. Divorce court is, in actuality, revenge court. At the time the parties need to do the most talking and communicating, they are encouraged by the court procedures and by their attorneys not to talk to each other or to the judge. These parties have demonstrated their difficulty in communication during the marriage since this was most likely one of the significant problems that led to the break-up of the marriage. Now they are being reinforced for having communication problems and their attorneys are helping them to perpetuate these. At a time when the system should be making every effort to help make this transition easier for the parties, they find themselves part of the system that wants to pit them against each other.

This type of system is most definitely not responsive or sensitive to the needs of the divorcing couple and certainly not sensitive to the needs of the children. There is no doubt that the goal of the divorce court is to settle issues. The judge will settle the issues of child custody, child and spousal support, visitation, and property division. The divorce will happen and the important matters will be taken care of even if both parties do not like the decision. However, the price that is paid for the divorce has the potential to be enormous. We have seen people use all of their savings in protracted court fights which never seem to end. Clients have told us horror stories over and over regarding the thousands of dollars in legal fees that are paid, and sometimes the tens and hundreds of thousands of dollars. In addition to this heavy insult the parties are dragged through a formalized system which makes no sense to them and which they do not understand and can cause them to end up as enemies. In addition, both the court and the parents have psychologically injured the children of the family. It seems that in such a progressive and highly technical age we would have the intellectual capacity to devise a system better than this. It would also appear that the dissolution should not have to require such enormous expenditure of funds and emotions. It would also appear that a system could be devised which would insure fairer outcomes and less of an adversarial approach. We constantly hear the same questions from our clients: Why can't it be fairer? Why does it have to be me against him? Why can't we try to work this out between ourselves? Why is it that I am on my fourth attorney and I still can't get what I want? If we have so much trouble communicating, why can't someone help us to get together? Why doesn't the divorce court system understand this? Why do we have to add a legal issue to the emotional and psychological trauma of splitting up? How come the judge takes so little time to hear our case?

It is easy to see that the divorce system is out of touch with its consumers' needs. If the parties were not so emotional at the time of the break-up, then there would hardly be divorce fights in divorce court. However, they are emotionally insecure and this is carried over to the courtroom. The legal system has no way to deal with the emotional issues so they are not taken into consideration when the divorce takes place. At a time when individuals are going through one of the most significant emotional traumas they will ever experience, they have very specific needs. Whether it is the death of a loved one, the loss of a job or the break-up of a marriage, we all need exactly the same experience. We need emotional support and understanding from those we care about. This is what we tend to look for when we go through a divorce. This can be supplied by a therapist or perhaps a family member, but not from the legal system and certainly not from an adversarial attorney. Once an individual goes to court, s/he is at a complete disadvantage. In court the parties are fragile, vulnerable, hurting, disappointed and very fearful. They only want understanding and sensitivity and no one really wants to be swept away in the legal system without full understanding of what is happening around them. The parties usually do not realize the fight they have let themselves in for and this only serves to again accentuate the fears and angers they feel. We have been in courtrooms where everyone, including the bailiff, looks as if they just want to cry. We have seen judges have to excuse themselves before they broke down and we have seen attorneys and clients broken and battered. Their own eyes and minds are clouded by the emotions they are feeling.

Most people who go to court believe that the judges are men and women who do not experience feelings in these matters. However, it is well known in the legal circles that the domestic court judges rapidly burn out and need long breaks from this type of case.

Judges in domestic court often take turns rotating through other court services to give themselves regular breaks. Without this approach we would simply use judges up too rapidly. They are people just like us, sensitive, anxious, often troubled by their own family difficulties, and very hard working.

The current legal system under which we operate does not have as one of its responsibilities the desire to show us much understanding or sensitivity. Attorneys tell the parties what they believe their rights are and what they might expect from the divorce court. They also help their client to look at the opposing spouse as an enemy. It is interesting that the couple put in many years working hard together to acquire advantages such as homes, furniture and cars. In divorce court they are given the attitude that they now have to fight over these items and they also have to fight over the children. The person who helped conceive the children out of love and desire, the person who helped to raise the children, now becomes a parent who was never really that good to the children. This person, who did homework with the children nightly, suddenly "never cared" about the children's needs, activities and welfare. This person is now to be denigrated and put upon. Attorneys write declarations for their clients which are exaggerations, often half-truths and sometimes completely false.

Although judges will tell the couple that they have to cooperate and that they have to be nice to each other for the children, the legal adversarial system encourages them to be enemies. Attorneys help the parties plan how to have custody and how to allow the other parent to have a minimum of visitation. The parents, angry and hurt, threaten each other and intimidate with the statement that if they cause all this trouble, they will never see the children again. Of course this entire dynamic makes no sense at all when one considers that this couple has focused their lives around their children.

Not only do the attorneys, judges and legislators perpetuate the current bad system, the people who utilize the system perpetuate it as well by not opting out of the struggle and by not voting for people who might be more sensitive. It appears as so basic and fundamental that all should know that a better system is necessary and available.

A more sensitive and responsive system would serve to benefit all divorcing couples and their children. This could also help the parties to be more responsible for their own individual behavior. With added insight the parties could begin to focus on those plans which would benefit the whole family unit and not just themselves.

There are many very important issues that must be looked at by the bar, the bench and the legislators in order to make positive and effective changes in the current system. The issues that need examination in order to develop a new, effective and different system are quite obvious. They include the following:

1. A way for the court to specifically avoid making husband and wife into adversaries;
2. A way for the court to encourage the participants to work together to achieve mutually beneficial cooperative solutions rather than to have winners and losers;
3. A way for attorneys and judges to have roles in encouraging the parties to talk and resolve their own problems rather than having to fight for everything;
4. A way for the court to insure that the parties will have the opportunity and the motivation to talk until they actually work out settlements for themselves;
5. A way for the court to specifically educate the parents regarding the effects of divorce on their children;
6. A way for the court to encourage the parties to work toward settlements which will specifically serve to benefit their children rather than themselves;
7. A way for the court to be open and fair with regard to the issues of money and support;
8. A way for the attorneys to be more interested in treating all the parties fairly rather than trying to take more than is fair or necessary from one spouse.

A new divorce system would have very different priorities. The current system of divorce in the United States has as its first priority simply getting the legal entanglement over and finished. It is not very concerned with what effect the divorce has on the wife, the husband or the children. The system does not at all make allowances for the parties to be able to transition from being married to being single. The system is also not very interested in the effects of the divorce outside the courtroom. The judge and the attorneys do not have to be concerned with this aspect, only the divorcing parties must consider the effects. The bitter divorces we see are reflected in society. They are manifested in: a large number of unhappy and clinically depressed children; high suicide rates among teenagers; increased pregnancy among teens; alcohol and drug abuse among parents and children; failed second and third marriages; and eventually, the future failure of the marriages of today's children. We are currently seeing second generation divorces and we see the children of divorce playing the same deadly games that they saw their parents play. It is obvious that our society is not successful in either marriage or divorce. All we are doing is becoming legally entangled and then legally untangled. This often is only for the moment in that so many divorced couples end up back in court numerous times as they fight over money and children.

    In an effort to re-design the divorce court we must decide on the first priority of a new system. The author believes that the first priority would have to be the recognition that divorce is such an emotionally and psychologically difficult time. It must first directly address the emotions that the husband and wife are actively experiencing and displaying before it can untangle this couple legally. The process and the feelings inherent in the actual breakup of the relationship must be recognized and brought to the surface. A new system will have to create an atmosphere which allows and assists the divorcing couple to work together to solve the problems that will now arise as a result of the divorce. This does not mean that they have to function without the assistance of attorneys, judges, mediators or therapists. It just means that the help they receive is structured differently than it is currently. The new system will offer a different type of help which specifically focuses on working together in a mediative or collaborative process rather than fighting each other in an adversarial process. The parties will meet not in a courtroom but in the chambers of a mediator or in the offices of collaborative lawyers. They will bring with them 20X20 pictures of their children which will be placed on the wall in front of them. All of their interactions from that moment will include and reference to the needs of the children in the pictures. The mediator and a therapist will then work with the couple in supportive psychotherapeutic interventions to help them to sort out the property and custody arrangements. The attorneys will participate in this process without being adversarial and be on call so that they can come and review the agreements which the parties, mediator and therapist have agreed to. The judge sits in chambers and does not have to hear these cases. S/he only has to sign the stipulation, smile, wish everyone luck and toss the hair of the little blonde guy with the smile on his face who is very happy to see his parents cooperating. This system would perpetuate integrity and honesty rather than stimulate manipulation and lying.

This type of divorce is undoubtedly far more beneficial than the current system. Currently, divorce leaves most people with a bitter impression of the legal system and a bitter impression of the ex-spouse. It is apparent that if the two parties had difficulties getting along in the marriage which prompted the need for the divorce, this will not suddenly heal all by itself. In fact, given the strictly adversarial system of the present, there is no doubt that the difficulties will only get worse. A great deal of money is spent in court and most of the time neither party feels that they were treated fairly. If the divorce court experience could be more supportive, more interested in understanding the needs of the parties as human beings with feelings, then the divorcing couple would be happier and better adjusted after the divorce was over. This will be beneficial for the children, for the future of the parenting relationships, and for maintaining a working relationship with the ex-spouse while perpetuating positive future relationships. If this were the case, a divorce situation would be therapeutic and would not be viewed as an experience of terror. If divorce court could be made to be a friendlier place, fears and bitterness would dissipate. The author has had experience with many clients who feared the divorce court more than they feared the break-up of their marriage. They had heard many negative stories from others who had gone through the process.

They had heard about how the court had completely fouled up people's lives which made the idea of court excessively threatening and fearful. A new system that does not establish the adversarial position but rather encourages working together would be highly desirable for all concerned. The new system would have to understand that divorcing couples may not want to work together so it will have to make certain that they do.

The author recommends that divorce court should be taken out of the present court system. A separate branch that is not founded on the traditional adversarial system would have to be created. The first benefit of this new system would be that the divorces would not have to compete with other civil and criminal matters for time, attention, courtrooms and judges. This could be similar to the manner in which many states handle injuries to workers on the job. Many states set up a separate worker's compensation court system that deals only with these problems in a very prescribed and special manner. The courts are not attached to the regular county court and the judges are specialists in this one area. They do not ordinarily hear other cases. In a similar manner a separate divorce system could also be established founded on healthier psychological principles.

The new divorce system as described would be cooperative, not adversarial. A new set of rules would be developed and new procedures would allow the divorcing couple to work together in a more informal setting with the mediators and therapists. Attorneys would work with each other and the couples in a joint effort to solve the problems, protect the children and distribute all assets and debts in a fair manner. Hearing officers or judges would be specially educated not only in the legal issues to be resolved but also in the psychological issues that divorcing couples ordinarily present. These judges would have the luxury of being able to take the time and energy to work individually with these couples to assist them in solving their problems or be available just to ratify their agreements. Techniques inherent in mediation and arbitration could be used successfully as everyone moves toward a common goal. These judges and hearing officers would be charged with the responsibility of overseeing each and every case to make certain that the matter was being handled properly by the attorneys and the divorcing couple. Mediators and counselors would help husband and wife through the emotional difficulty of divorce. These professionals would also help the couple to resolve any child custody disagreements. These professionals would be licensed by the state to do these jobs specifically. The divorcing couple would be able to access the entire divorce package at a rate far below the current standard fees and this would assist the parties to maintain their financial integrity as well. The mental health professionals would work not only with the parents but also with the children to help them to resolve their problems and to help make the transition easier for them. The divorce court would take an interest in making certain that this couple was better adjusted and better able to cope with their future life as single people. Divorce court would still be charged with the job of helping the couple to untangle legally. However, this would be done through a process combining healthy legal and psychological principles which would help the couple to deal with their negative and bitter emotions so that the desire for fighting and revenge would not persist as it does at the present. Keep in mind that the judge, to whom the case has been assigned, would always oversee the progress of the divorce process. It is this judge that will have to sign off on any court orders and the final judgment, even if the case never goes into the courtroom.

When Martha decided that it was time for her to file for a divorce from Todd, she arranged to meet with her attorney whose job is to prepare the initial papers. This will get them into the divorce court schedule. Todd will be notified immediately by Martha's attorney and he will be at the filing with or without an attorney. Todd and Martha's case will be handled individually and not in a courtroom full of onlookers and others waiting to check in or be heard by the judge. A mediator and therapist will be present and the services of an accountant consultant will also be requested. They will then have a joint meeting during which they will come to agreement on a custody/visitation schedule. The next meeting will deal with finances so that neither party is left with no money. The parties will be instructed to prepare a comprehensive list of assets and debts so that these can be dealt with at the next meeting. They will be told how to follow these rules and procedures in a therapeutic session and it will be impressed on them that this is a far more effective way to function rather than to fight for everything. Counselors will be present to help each of them handle the emotional trauma of the divorce. They will be taught how to speak and communicate more effectively with each other. This will all be done in a rapid succession of meetings so that a great deal of work can be accomplished in a relatively short period of time.

This is a very different and far better method than the one currently used in our traditional court system. These concepts are not necessarily unique to the author. They are obvious and many mental health professionals and sophisticated attorneys have recommended similar systems. It makes good common sense – a function that is all but lost in these times.

If Martha wanted to file for divorce in the current system, she would have her attorney prepare the papers which would then be served on Todd, probably at his place of employment so that he could be maximally embarrassed. He would hire his attorney and at some time in the future they would see a court mediator who would most likely make no recommendation. They would then come to court to wait for hours, vie for the judge's attention and try to get a hearing even though they were calendared for this particular time. The court sessions would drag on as the judge was continually interrupted by juries coming in, papers to sign, and hysterical people begging for emergency hearings. Eventually they would come to an order from the judge regarding custody and visitation as well as support and a division of property. In the meanwhile, which would certainly be months, Martha may need support and Todd may not be helping out at all. Martha may try to use the children to get what she wants from Todd and a battle will ensue with the children getting hurt psychologically. Under the current system, these issues would eventually be resolved but it would involve several months of negotiations, declarations, perhaps a psychological evaluation of the entire family, testimony in court, hearings, numerous letters going back and forth between attorneys, hostility, and the judge getting very tired of seeing this intractable couple in court. It is an extremely slow, often agonizing and frustrating process that takes far too long and is far too impersonal and very threatening to everyone's integrity.

Under the new system which we are proposing, these activities as described above would not take place at all. The parties would meet with sensitive people who offer them their full attention in a cooperative and positive manner. The couple would not have to wait for an indefinite amount of time to have these very important questions settled.

There is no doubt that this will take very well trained people exerting much concentrated time and energy. It will take on a completely new attitude and atmosphere than our current court system. However, it can be accomplished. Divorce court would have to be renamed. It can be operating every day, all day with specially trained legal and psychological professionals who have been highly schooled and are experts in the area of legal procedure, family systems and conflict resolution techniques. They will not be competing with other legal cases and they will therefore have enough time to handle each and every case. The more that can be resolved in the first extended meeting, the less often the couple will have to appear in court. The state should have an interest in the health and welfare of its citizens. If this is so, we can no longer hide our heads in the sand. We must recognize how poorly the current system is operating and how damaging it is to families and individuals. It is to the benefit of the citizens as well as the court system to be certain that enough appropriately educated and sophisticated psychological personnel will be employed to make this system run smoothly.

It is very likely that this system will cost more money that the current system. However, in the long run, this system will save money for all concerned. Currently divorcing couples must pay extremely high sums for attorneys. In addition, even though they must accept a mandatory mediation, they must also pay for it in the current court system. Therefore, if they were to pay the same amount for a system which would enhance their lives instead of hurt them further, this would improve the quality of life for all concerned. Husbands and wives would leave each other on friendlier terms and would be less likely to re-appear for thirty-two contempt hearings as we so often see now. The effect on children would be far more positive. They would see their parents getting along well and working on a cooperative, healthy, joint parenting arrangement which would truly be in their best interests. This will make for better adjusted children, less delinquency and fewer relationship difficulties. This will ultimately cost the state less in time and money and will clearly result in healthier and happier citizens. The current system cries out for change and should not be perpetuated.

CHAPTER 10
REFLECTIONS ON RELATIONSHIPS

There are a number of significant philosophical questions that man has asked from the beginning of time. Of all of these issues, perhaps the two most significant and difficult questions we ask ourselves involve the meaning of life and the meaning of love. Great philosophers wrestle with the answers to what goes into feelings of love and no definitive information has ever been forthcoming. We have all experienced many different kinds of love. These feelings enter into brief as well as longer lasting relationships. There are love feelings for immediate family relationships with parents or children, more distant relative relationships such as aunt and uncle or cousin, intense boyfriend-girlfriend relationships or husband and wife. Each of these relationships is special, unique and based in some form of 'love' feelings. It is clear that the most intriguing love circumstances and the most difficult to understand, is the one which leads us into marriage. We write poems and songs glorifying this experience but we cannot define it other than operationally as it takes place. The extent of this commitment is unrelated to anything else we can possibly enter into. It is expected to outlast all other interests and all other relationships.

There are certainly volumes and volumes written about marital relationships and, for all we know, we have discovered that we actually know very little.

In this book we have attempted to open the reader to the issues inherent in divorce so that the reader will be able to look at the process of divorce with a new and healthier attitude. This new attitude will lead to different perspectives and new positive ways to deal with these difficulties in life. Divorce exists only because marriage exists. It is clear that no dissertation on divorce can be complete without addressing the issues of how relationships and specifically marriage works or falls apart.

Many researchers and writers agree that the love relationship that leads to marriage arises from a basic human need to experience intensity in intimacy, romance, sharing, and the formation of a private human connection. We long for these experiences throughout our lives. We look for prospective partners in the produce department of our local super market as well as every other place. We seek out prospective partners and relationships from the moment we begin to understand and identify feelings. We meet many people and develop many relationships at different levels. We continually seek out that level which will tell us that this is the individual with whom we want to establish a permanent commitment. Initially, when we begin relationships we consider the possibility of emotional closeness. This produces excitement, thrills, positive feelings of reinforcement as well as an awakening of sexuality. As these feelings build, the closeness develops and we find ourselves talking and thinking about marriage. In most situations this is premature and probably not really appropriate.

The relationship remains a mystery and takes a great deal of time and thought before it really develops to the point of seriousness.

Not all romantic relationships end in marriage. In many, we find that the person with whom we are involved is not the right person to marry. The desire to make that lifelong commitment is not there and this eventually forces the relationship to come to an end. The author has been confronted time after time with situations where the parties married long before the relationship had come to a point of maturity and commitment. Had they waited, they most likely would not have married. Marriage can be forced because of cultural needs or fantasy expectations or desires for security. These are the classic circumstances that lead to future failures. It is possible for the need to marry to actually interfere with the normal growth and development of the relationship. If the need was not so strong and culturally fed, it is possible that the relationship would simply run its course and end. It is apparent from the excessive divorce rate in this country that at least half of the marriages that take place are immature. We are at the point where at least as many marriages come to a legal end as survive. This clearly points to the fact that people do not consider seriously enough all of the ramifications prior to marrying. They may not be truthfully discussing the entire notion of commitment and the possible consequences. Many people are swept away to the altar on the wings of bliss. When the dust settles and they realize what they have done, they do not always like or understand it. The true nature of the relationship should be thoroughly discussed. In this way it can be made clear to both parties as to whether this is a potential marital relationship or not.

     A romantic relationship that brings love, joy, intimacy, and sharing may be experienced without the act of marriage. Marriage itself is not what releases these feelings between two people. These deep important feelings exist in the relationship. The essence of the relationship should not be confused with the form of the relationship. The essence is the love and the joy. The form may exist as a long distance relationship where the parties do not have a great deal of contact. It can also exist in a relationship where the parties live together or also in a more traditional marriage. The form does not provide the essence. A couple does not have a mediocre, unfulfilling relationship, then get married and suddenly begin experiencing intimacy, love and joy. Because our societal values, our romantic notions and our mothers have told us so many times that this intense essence will be experienced in marriage, we often marry without truly examining the relationship and its essence. Often we simply do not have enough understanding of what we want from the other person and of what we are willing to offer to another in a close and intimate, loving relationship.

It is important to study and observe why we tend to marry too early in a relationship. Frequently, we do not allow the relationship to take its natural course to see if it will ultimately lead to marriage. If this is where our destiny is with our partner, it will most likely happen at some point. Unfortunately, we frequently succumb to societal pressures from family, friends, and also from our own need to hurry and make things happen. We have grown up with the rules about when we should marry, when children should be born and how we should live. We have a strong internal desire to be with someone to mate and to nest. Just as nature abhors a vacuum, humans tend to abhor being alone. There are always fears that one of the parties will leave or that no one better can be found. Therefore, our societal training teaches us to lock up the relationship by making commitments early and also by asking our partners for commitments very early. We have the view that marriage will be forever and that the form of the relationship will dictate the essence and that everything will miraculously take care of itself. We tend to deny problem areas because it is easier to be blind to fears than to address them and possibly have the relationship disappear. Eventually, when the problem areas do come to the surface, they have to be examined. This is the time that many divorces result. Frequently, the author has had many discussions with clients who have so regretted marrying. They state "If only I'd waited". They explain that they do not know why they rushed into marriage and they do not know why they could not allow the relationship to progress and run its natural course. These people felt that if they had done this, the relationship might simply have ended at some point and the marriage would not have taken place. It is interesting to note that these rules are being challenged and society is making changes daily. Younger members of society are waiting far longer before they commit to another person, and they are experiencing more relationships than past generational members did. It is difficult to know whether this is positive or negative since the divorce rate has remained about the same for a number of years. However, it is entirely possible that the high divorce statistics come from much earlier marriages.

Marriage is a curious phenomenon because it demands a great deal of logistical planning. When one person lives alone and has few responsibilities, life may be lonely but it is relatively simple. Plans can be made, changed, broken and re-made and no one else has to be consulted. When two people marry: they live together; own things together; have children together; get life insurance for each other; plan holidays together; and try to blend two basic families who do not know each other. This may include: children; ex-spouses; mothers and fathers; sisters and brothers. Suddenly there are continuous decisions that have to be made every minute of the day. This logistical, administrative part of the marriage always takes both time and energy away from the essence of the marriage. When we become plagued with tasks, bills, things, children's needs, appointments, clogged drains and exploding hot water heaters, we lose closeness and intimacy. We keep putting intimacy on hold until it stops being at the top of the list. It slides down quickly and before we know it, we have lost the motivation to be intimate. Closeness and contact suffer as life is taken up with many extraneous details. The bonds of closeness, joy and love begin to slowly fade as they are replaced with details and more and more logistical considerations. When we see these things happening we begin to ask the questions of what happened and where did the love go?

Although it is difficult before marriage to even know that these problems will exist, they do need to be thought of and considered. If the bond that is established between two people has a strong foundation of love, intimacy and sharing in the relationship before the marriage, then they can rely on this foundation. Hopefully, it will be strong enough to support all of the inane details that come about in a marriage so that attention will not waiver from the true essence of the relationship. If this true essence is carefully cultivated and appreciated before marriage, a strong foundation will be created that can always be used to fall back on when extra strength is needed. If this foundation is not well established and firm, there will be inevitable problems when the marriage hits difficult times. When this happens the parties begin to re-examine their relationship and the needs they wish this relationship to meet. One or both parties decide that it is time for divorce if there is no adequate foundation to build upon. When expectations are not met it becomes apparent that the work of the couple in examining the relationships prior to their marriage was not done effectively.

There is a small percentage of couples that do take the time to examine their relationship before marriage. They learn about each other and they are aware of the potential for personal growth within the relationship. They are better prepared for the difficulties which will be encountered. These are people who have not forced the love relationship into the form of marriage before it was ready. Instead, they have allowed the relationship to dictate its own form. Just as a river flows, relationships flow and they have to be left alone to move to their natural end point. Sometimes we want so badly for the relationship to be something other than what it is that we close our eyes to the obvious flaws. Often couples will be more concerned with the outcome of the relationship than they are in simply living the relationship. The need to force everything into a marriage is negative and destructive. Often we become more concerned to make relationships end in marriage than we are with whether or not the relationship is right for both parties. The mistaken idea that we will be able to satisfy needs for security in inappropriate marriages always takes its toll.

The marital commitment is very strong. It is a commitment to remain together and to do all that can be done to promote love, understanding, intimacy and sharing. A marital relationship is all encompassing. It permits us to have another individual with whom we can share hopes, desires, fears and anxieties, and private secrets. The individual whom we select to share these aspects of self is a very special person. This requires a deep connection.

It is interesting to see that so many people are so willing to rush into marriage without closely examining the partner and the essence of the relationship. When we are led into marriage by our fears and anxieties we lose track of the need for a deep commitment to be with the partner in love and truth. This is partly what is meant by the statement that each person must take responsibility for his/her role in the marriage and perhaps in the eventual divorce.

It is conceivable that the divorce rate could drop dramatically with more emphasis on the pre-marriage examination of the relationship. If the natural flow of the relationship is permitted to take its own course without a premature forcing of marriage, perhaps deeper and more truthful commitments could be made. Even if divorce were to take place in the future, it would most certainly be less bitter and less emotionally scarring for the individuals concerned. People who see the natural flow of their relationship leading to marriage also see when the natural flow leads to divorce. Divorce court as it is presently constituted, is not an attractive option because these particular parties do not seem to have to be so punitive to their spouses for not being the person they wanted. This couple will no doubt experience genuine pain and disappointment in their divorce, but it is certain that they will handle it better. In addition, the data demonstrates that these people will have an easier time making new subsequent relationships.

Relationships teach us about ourselves, our strengths and weaknesses. Within a positive and nurturing relationship we can become healthy and fulfilled. In order to do this, we need to examine why we are in the relationship and what it truly means for both of the partners. They wish to share a common ground of commitment, love, trust, truthfulness. Sharing and growth, perhaps this marriage will work and not end in divorce. Because this is what every couple wants, it is wise to spend a good deal of time carefully examining what the relationship means. This will reveal if this partner is truly someone with whom one can spend a life. To open our eyes, ears and heart as wide as possible is good advice. In this way we can grow to experience and to know the essence of the relationship and commitment that the two people actually have. This is far better than moving too rapidly into marriage without adequate awareness and insight regarding a prospective partner.

Over the course of a life we will have many experiences, meet many new and different people and undergo numerous changes. This is the nature of life. Over the course of years our opinions and beliefs, our likes and dislikes, and our basic philosophies will modify and change. We will undoubtedly change careers, ideas and even geographical locations. We experience many deep joys and many deep sorrows. As they enter our lives they change our lives. We are not the same person at thirty or forty or fifty that we were at twenty. In fact, over the years we even change the manner in which we define and value our relationships. If we are involved in close, intimate and romantic relationships both of the partners make changes and they have to offer each other the opportunity and freedom to be different. The relationship cannot endure unless the foundations remain solid and the friendships remain intact. This requires continuous re-defining of the meaning of the relationship and looking very closely at the person with whom the commitment has been made as well as looking deep within our own selves.

Divorce is certainly a traumatic event, but it is also an excellent teacher. It awakens us to the realities of relationships and also to what we truly want for ourselves. It can have the benefit of making us more aware and it can lead to much more depth in relationships. It can lead to more personal growth and awareness and this will ultimately lead to a more fulfilling life. As we have noted, divorce can be a way of expressing vengeance, punishment and hate because the spouse did not live up to expectations. It can also lead us to learn how to experience, in a new relationship, the intensity of joy, love and intimacy. If a divorce occurs, the parties can still get along and can utilize this experience for positive and effective growth. Some relationships are meant to last a lifetime, while others are not.

Divorcing with sanity is very possible if the parties want it. If they do not, very little can be done short of ordering them to cooperate or beating them into submission. In this book we have clearly demonstrated the existing procedures, the pitfalls, and the strong needs for change that the system requires. It is now up to the reader to do all those things and take all those steps to maintain sanity and divorce with the least amount of pain and suffering. The author prays that the divorcing parties will heed these messages.

About the Author

Rick Rabbin is currently a family law practitioner in Ventura County, California. He has previously practiced law in several other counties in California and operated a mediation business in Portland, Oregon. While in Oregon, he worked with a State Assemblywoman to introduce legislation that created a Task Force that revised Oregon divorce laws to make them more equitable. He offers experienced representation and expertise in the area of Family Law. He also handles mediation cases and collaborative law divorce cases. He is past president of the Ventura County Family Law Bar Association. A graduate of the Pepperdine School of Law and member of the California Bar Association since 1974, Mr. Rabbin has been in practice over 35 years. Whether representing a client in court, mediating on his or her behalf, or offering family law advice on an hourly basis, Mr. Rabbin's client relationship is distinguished by his careful listening to the client's desires and goals; he always takes the time to fully include the client in all solution strategies. This book is derived from the many hours spent with clients in his office, in the courtroom and with judges and other attorneys in litigating and resolving family law cases.

Thousand Oaks Office:
171 East Thousand Oaks Blvd., Suite 101
Thousand Oaks, CA 91360

Telephone: 805.449.1777

Web: www.richardsrabbin.com

www.ingramcontent.com/pod-product-compliance
Lightning Source LLC
Chambersburg PA
CBHW070756100426
42742CB00012B/2151